D0982667

Japanese Landlords

Published under the auspices of
THE CENTER FOR JAPANESE AND KOREAN STUDIES
University of California, Berkeley

ANN WASWO

Japanese Landlords

THE DECLINE OF A RURAL ELITE

UNIVERSITY OF CALIFORNIA PRESS

Berkeley • Los Angeles • London

University of California Press
Berkeley and Los Angeles, California

University of California Press, Ltd.
London, England

ISBN 0-520-03217-9
Library of Congress Catalog Card Number: 76-7771
Printed in the United States of America

Contents

List of Tables

Acknowledgments

In writing the dissertation on which this book is based, I benefited greatly from the guidance of two individuals: Thomas Smith, my adviser at Stanford University, who first brought rural Japan to my attention, and Ronald Dore, whom I have never met but whose published work on the landlords pointed me in many of the right directions as I pursued what often proved an elusive subject. I owe thanks, too, to Furushima Toshio, Tōbata Seiichi, Matsuo Takeo, Baba Akira, Taniguchi Sumio, Kubo Yasuo, Saitō Isamu and Nishida Yoshiaki, who generously shared their knowledge with me during two periods of research in Japan.

Many colleagues in the United States aided me in the final stages of preparing this manuscript. In particular I would like to thank Jane Yamazaki, Terry MacDougall, Gary Allinson, Thomas Havens, Irwin Scheiner, Richard Smethurst and Tom Kessinger for their helpful comments and criticisms. I also appreciate the financial support I received from the Fulbright-Hays fellowship program, the Japan Foundation, and the University of Virginia, as well as the permission of Princeton University Press to include portions of my essay, "The Origins of Tenant Unrest," originally published in *Japan in Crisis: Essays on Taishō Democracy* (1974), edited by Bernard S. Silberman and H. D. Harootunian.

Acknowledgments

Finally, to one of the three severest critics of writing I have ever encountered, my husband Rick, I apologize for the few remaining nouns that are used as adjectives and offer thanks for the patience he usually displayed in pointing out the error of my ways.

Charlottesville, 1976   A.W.

CHAPTER ONE

Introduction

"The landlord is the parent tree of the land. The tenants, like ivy, coil around his trunk and are protected from the weather." So observed Amano Fujio in 1920 in a book about landlord-tenant relations in Japan.[1] In little more than a decade, however, his metaphor had been reversed by a new generation of Japanese scholars who were influenced both by Marxist thought and by the appearance during the 1920s of an organized tenant movement and an increasing number of tenancy disputes. Now tenants were portrayed as the tree trunk giving life to the Japanese countryside. Landlords had become the ivy—or, more sinisterly, parasites—performing no useful functions themselves but simply living off their tenants and depriving them of sustenance. It had been thus, these scholars asserted, since at least the late nineteenth century. Landlords were "not only contemporary enemies," who opposed much-needed reforms of the tenancy system, "but historical obstacles to progress as well."[2]

This latter view, expressed most forcefully by Hirano Yoshitarō in the early 1930s, has prevailed, at least until recently, in most

1. Amano Fujio, *Nōson shakai mondai: jinushi to kosakunin* (Tokyo, 1920), p. 18.
2. Ronald Dore, "The Meiji Landlord: Good or Bad?," *Journal of Asian Studies* 18 (May 1959): 345.

Japanese scholarship and in the relatively few English-language studies of rural society in prewar Japan. Wakukawa Seiyei, for example, observed in 1946 that

> much of the continued dominance of feudal remnants that permeate every aspect of Japanese life finds an economic basis in the semi-feudal tenancy system. Tenancy has epitomized everything reactionary and retrogressive in Japan since the Meiji Restoration.[3]

To Andrew Grad, the poverty of tenant farmers in the 1930s was "not a result of stagnation in agriculture, [or of] the absence of will on the part of peasants . . . to improve their lot."[4] In large measure, it was the handiwork of landlords, whose activities "tended to preserve feudal-like conditions in the villages."

> These landlords—lately merchants, owners of inns and brothels, masters of road repair crews, and persons of similar status . . . began [in the 1870s] to emulate the former lords whom they had observed in their youth. They built mansions . . . formed marriage alliances with famous old families, aspired to leading local political positions, made donations to the temples . . . acquired concubines, and received as their due the respects paid by their tenants. In this way the atmosphere of the pre-Restoration village was preserved up to the Pacific War.[5]

More recently, Barrington Moore has concluded:

> In Japan the advent of the modern world brought with it an increase in agricultural production, but mainly through the creation of a class of small property owners who extracted rice from the peasantry through a mixture of capitalist and feudal mechanisms. The peasants subsisted in large numbers very close to the margin of physical survival. . . . In return what did this new landlord class contribute to Japanese society? As far as I am able to judge the record, it offered neither the artistic culture nor the security of earlier rulers in the countryside, indeed scarcely more than pious proto-fascist sentiments.[6]

3. Wakukawa Seiyei, "The Japanese Farm Tenancy System," in *Japan's Prospect*, ed. D.G. Haring, (Cambridge, Massachusetts, 1946), p. 116.

4. Andrew Grad, *Land and Peasant in Japan: An Introductory Survey* (New York, 1952), p. 15.

5. Ibid., p. 23.

ᗞ. Barrington Moore, *Social Origins of Dictatorship and Democracy: Lord and Peasant in the Making of the Modern World* (Boston, 1967), pp. 286-87.

Such harsh appraisals of landlords in the 1930s and immediate postwar era no doubt facilitated the land reform of 1947-50 which virtually eliminated tenancy—and landlords—in Japan. Had the forces of good and evil in the countryside not been so clearly identified, it might have proven much more difficult to effect such a sweeping reform. But as is so often the case, these same appraisals, however useful as a basis for action, have made for poor history: they present a seriously oversimplified view of landlords and their role in rural society.

This study will focus on Japanese landlords in the years from 1868 to the late 1930s. The span of time may appear somewhat arbitrary—after all, there were landlords before 1868 and after the outbreak of the Pacific War—but I believe it constitutes a major phase not only in the modern history of Japan but in the history of Japanese landlords as well. The Meiji Restoration of 1868 and the land settlement which followed it brought about important changes in the status of landlords, providing them with hitherto unparalleled opportunities to profit from leasing land and enhancing their authority in both tenancy relations and village life. For the next half century or so they functioned as the dominant elite of the countryside and exerted considerable influence in national affairs as well. In the early 1900s, however, their position began to deteriorate. The governmental bureaucracy which had once relied heavily on landlords to mobilize popular support for the programs and policies of the new regime became increasingly able to handle its own affairs and to reach the rural population directly. Once counted among the very wealthiest groups in the nation, landlords were soon rivaled and then surpassed by men involved in commerce and industry. Businessmen and professional politicians successfully challenged their position of influence within political parties.

But it was in rural society itself, the special preserve of landed interests, that the most significant erosion of their status and influence occurred. The tenancy disputes that erupted throughout parts of Japan in the years after World War I not only caused landlords economic losses, but also revealed to them that the days of their unquestioned authority in rural affairs, of their ability to count on the deference and submissiveness of their tenants, were over.[7] An additional, and not entirely unrelated, problem they faced in the 1920s and 1930s was chronic agricultural depression. Increasingly landlords lamented that there were no profits to be made from leasing land and, save for selling off their holdings, no solution to their difficulties. Well before the imposition of controls on rents and prices during the Pacific War and the execution of the postwar land reform, landlords were in serious decline.

My particular concern in this study will be to account for the problems landlords faced at the "rice roots" level in their relations with their tenants. In my view, more was involved in bringing about tenant restiveness and protest than the simple dialectic between the forces of oppression and liberation that is portrayed in much of the existing literature. Undoubtedly there were landlords (though I believe their number has been exaggerated) who after the turn of the century had come

to regard the villages as worthless places and farming as miserable work. . . . While tenants weeding the fields expose their backs to the scorching sun, landlords slip on *haori* and romp around on bicycles, their destination the village office, the temple or the police station, where they play checkers all day.[8]

Clearly the high rents in kind which landlords collected, generally amounting to half the crop, produced resentment—and at times real suffering—among tenants. The spread of literacy, a result of the universal education system established in the late nineteenth century, not only lessened the dependence of tenants on their landlords but also made at least some tenants more responsive to the exhortations of left-wing intellectuals who called in the 1920s and

---

7. For a discussion of tenant restiveness, see Ann Waswo, "The Origins of Tenant Unrest," in *Japan in Crisis: Essays on Taishō Democracy,* eds. Bernard S. Silberman and H. D. Harootunian (Princeton, 1974), pp. 374-94.

8. Ono Shōzō, "Jinushi shoshi ni hansei o unagasu," in *Nōson mondai jōhō,* Aichi ken nōji kyōkai, (Nagoya, n.d.), quoted in Aichi ken nōchi shi hensen iinkai, ed., *Aichi ken nōchi shi* 1 (Nagoya 1957): 454.

1930s for elimination of "semi-feudal parasitic landlord exploiters."[9]
But landlords were not simply doomed by "history" to decline. Of
key importance in causing the erosion of their position was their very
capacity for innovation. Landlords lost the respect and obedience of
their tenants less because they opposed progress than because they
promoted it.

It is difficult indeed to fit Japanese landlords to the modern
stereotype of landed elites. With few exceptions they were commoners, not aristocrats. Although they enjoyed social prestige, they
possessed no inherited privileges or rights. Nor were they wastrels.
Most landlords lived comfortably, and a few, elegantly. But a large
proportion of their wealth was used productively, not dissipated in
conspicuous display. They were actively concerned with improving
agriculture and village life. Again in contrast to the stereotype,
there is little evidence that they found trade and industry repugnant.
Although their status as an elite was based on the ownership of
land, many landlords also invested in the non-agricultural sector—
primarily in banking, railroads and manufacturing. Others played
a more direct role in the non-agricultural economy, as owners and
managers of such enterprises as sake breweries, mines or textile
mills. The sons of landed families formed a disproportionate share
of Japan's business elite.[10]

Their "uncharacteristic" behavior brought landlords immediate
monetary rewards, but in the long run it undercut their position in
rural society. The agricultural improvements landlords sponsored—
for example, irrigation projects to lessen the danger of flooding

9. The phrase, the longest and harshest denunciation of landlords I have en-
countered, is Hirano Yoshitarō's, quoted in Dore, "The Meiji Landlord," p. 345.
For discussion of the effects of education on tenants, see Hayashi Chūtarō, "Kosaku
mondai ni kansuru kōsatsu," *Teikoku nōkai hō* 11 (November 1921): 26-31; Ronald
Dore, *Land Reform in Japan* (London, 1959), pp. 54-55; Waswo, "Origins of
Tenant Unrest," pp. 377-79.

10. Thomas Smith, "Landlords' Sons in the Business Elite," *Economic Development and Cultural Change* 9 (October 1960): 93-108. See also G. Ranis, "Financing
of Japanese Economic Development," *Economic History Review* 9 (April 1959): 447.
For a general discussion of landed elites, see Everett Hagen, *On the Theory of
Social Change: How Economic Growth Begins* (Homewood, Illinois, 1962),
pp. 77-80.

and drought—reduced tenant dependence on them for aid in time of distress. To the extent that landlords became involved in non-agricultural affairs, it became more difficult for them to concern themselves with day-to-day village life. But it was precisely upon the landlords' role as economic protectors and social leaders of their communities that their legitimacy—the acceptance by tenants and other villagers of their elite status and wealth—had been based. Landlords had not simply extracted rents from tenants; in return they had provided services which tenants valued. When those services were no longer needed or no longer provided, there was little left to check tenant resentment and hostility.

Before turning to a detailed discussion of the ways in which landlords contributed, unwittingly to be sure, to their own undoing, I should acknowledge the necessary limitations of this study. One can divide landlords into two general types: non-cultivating landlords who rented out all or almost all their land to tenants, and cultivating landlords who farmed a substantial part of their land themselves and rented out the rest.[11] There is no way of knowing, however, precisely how many landlords of either type there were at any given time. Although a few surveys of the largest landlords in the country, those owning 50 *chō* or more of land, do exist,[12] no attempt was ever made to survey landlords as a whole. One must rely, therefore, on rough approximations of their number.

To obtain a figure for non-cultivating landlords, one must employ the statistics on land ownership and farm households compiled

11. Ōuchi Tsutomu, *Nōgyō mondai* (Tokyo, 1961), p. 206.
12. 1 *chō* (10 *tan*) equals 2.45 acres, or roughly 1 hectare. For information on the largest landlords in the country, see Nōshōmushō, nōmukyoku, "Gojitchōbu ijō no kōchi o shoyū suru ōjinushi ni kansuru chōsa (1921)," Nōrinshō, nōmukyoku, "Gojitchōbu ijō no kōchi o shoyū suru ōjinushi ni kansuru chōsa (1925)," and "Gojitchōbu ijō no ōjinushi meibo (1924)," reprinted in Nōgyō hattatsu shi chōsa kai, ed., *Nihon nōgyō hattatsu shi* 7 (Tokyo, 1955): 671–774; Nōchi kaikaku kiroku iinkai, ed., *Nōchi kaikaku tenmatsu gaiyō* (Tokyo, 1951), pp. 801–22; Shibutani Ryuichi and Ishiyama Shōjirō, "Meiji chūki no jinushi meibo," *Tochi seido shigaku*, No. 30 (June 1966), pp. 54–70; Shibutani Ryūichi, ed., *Jinushi meibo shiryō shozai mokuroku* (Tokyo, 1963); Ohashi Hirō, "Gojitchōbu ijō ōjinushi chōsa oyobi meibo no mondai," *Chihō shi kenkyū*, No. 52 (1961), pp. 51–59.

annually between 1908 and 1940 by the Ministry of Agriculture. By subtracting the number of landowning farmers (both owner-cultivators, who owned more than 90 percent of the land they cultivated, and part-tenants, who owned less than 90 percent but more than 10 percent of the land they cultivated) from the total number of landowners, a figure for non-cultivating landowners—that is, non-cultivating landlords—is produced. It is generally recognized, however, that the land ownership statistics, the basis for this calculation, were themselves inflated. Since the data were collected by village agricultural associations only for the land within their own jurisdictions, an individual with land in two or more villages was listed in the final statistics as two or more owners. It follows, then, that the number of non-cultivating landlords computed from the above total was also inflated.[13] In all probability, therefore, the actual number of non-cultivating landlords was lower than the estimates given in Table 1.

TABLE 1.
Estimated Number of Non-Cultivating Landlords
1908–1937 (including Hokkaido)

Year	Total number of landowners (A)	Number of landowning farmers (B)	Number of non-cultivating landlords (A – B)
1908	4,936,769	3,916,630	1,020,139
1917	4,853,042	3,933,655	919,387
1927	4,929,640	3,986,822	942,818
1937	5,057,691	3,990,747	1,066,944

Source: Chūō bukka tōsei kyōryoku kaigi, *Nihon ni okeru nōgyō keiei narabi ni tochi shoyū no hensen ni kansuru sankō shiryō* (Tokyo, 1943), pp. 13, 16, 22, 30.

13. For an excellent analysis of the land ownership statistics and other problems in determining the number of non-cultivating landlords, see Tōbata Seiichi, *Nōchi o meguru jinushi to nōmin* (Tokyo, 1947), pp. 9–32.

For cultivating landlords, only one set of figures—for the year 1940—exists for the prewar period. The data are shown in Table 2, with the estimated number of non-cultivating landlords the same year. At this time there were 666,000 cultivating landlords, roughly 40 percent of the total number of landlords. As will be discussed later, cultivating landlords probably constituted a larger percentage of all landlords earlier in the century.

A second complication in discussing landlords arises from the great differences among them in the area of land they owned. It is generally agreed that a holding of at least 5 to 10 *chō* of land was required for an individual to support himself and his family solely on income from tenant rents.[14] Yet most landlord holdings were considerably smaller—although Amano could write of "parent trees" of the land, Burke would have been hard-pressed to locate any "great oaks." In 1940, for example, 1,639,000 of an estimated 1,738,000 landlords owned less than 5 *chō* and depended on other sources of income—employment in the village office, schoolteaching, or part-time farming—to make ends meet. Their way of life and standard of living differed, one may safely assume, from the roughly 100,000 landlords who owned more than 5 *chō,* and even more so, from the approximately 3,000 landlords at the top of the scale who owned from 50 to a reported high of 1,840 *chō.*[15] In many studies these smaller, "petty" landlords have been excluded, and attention focused only on larger, "landlord-like" landlords. Although this exclusion creates a more manageable sample, it prevents consideration of some of the important differences in economic behavior and social role between the many small and few large landlords in Japan. In this study both categories will be considered.

14. Araki Moriaki, "Jinushi sei no tenkai," in *Iwanami kōza Nihon rekishi* 16 (Tokyo, 1962): 81; Dore, *Land Reform,* p. 29; Kurt Singer, "Landlords and Tenant Farmers of Japan," *Economic Record* 23 (December 1947): 247.

15. Tōbata Seiichi, *Nihon shihonshugi no keisei sha* (Tokyo, 1964), p. 133; by the same author, *Ichi nōsei gakuto no kiroku* (Tokyo, 1947), pp. 118-19. Landlords owning 50 *chō* or more were concentrated in Hokkaido, the Tohoku district, and Niigata Prefecture. See *Nōchi kaikaku tenmatsu gaiyō,* pp. 803-5.

TABLE 2.

Estimated Number of Cultivating and Non-Cultivating Landlords,
1940 (including Hokkaido)

Area of land owned	Number of cultivating landlords	Number of non-cultivating landlords	Total	Area of tenanted land
5 *chō* or more	25,000 (25.2%)	74,000 (74.8%)	99,000 (100%)	1,284,000 *chō* (46.4%)
1–5 *chō*	141,000 (49.1%)	146,000 (50.9%)	287,000 (100%)	1,119,000 *chō* (40.4%)
Less than 1 *chō*	500,000 (37.0%)	852,000 (63.0%)	1,352,000 (100%)	364,000 *chō* (13.2%)
Total	666,000 (38.3%)	1,072,000 (61.7%)	1,738,000 (100%)	2,767,000 *chō* (100%)

Source: Nōrinshō, *Nōchi mondai ni kansuru tōkei shiryō* (Tokyo, 1946), p. 16, quoted in Ōuchi Tsutomu, *Nōgyō mondai* (Tokyo, 1961), p. 207.

Nor was the amount of land landlords owned the only source of diversity among them. What kind of land it was and where it was located were also important variables. A landlord owning only upland fields, for example, on which rents were usually lower than on rice fields, generally was not as well off as a landlord with a holding of the same size in paddy.[16] Similarly, a landlord owning land in southwestern Japan, where a favorable climate made double-cropping possible and enabled him to charge slightly higher rents, was better off than a landlord with an identical holding in the single-crop region of the northeast.

A final complication to be noted at this point arises from the scarcity of detailed information of a non-quantitative sort about landlords and landlord-tenant relations. Some materials, including the original data for two government surveys of nationwide tenancy practices and agricultural conditions in the 1880s, were lost when

16. Ono Takeo, *Nōson shi*, vol. 9 of *Gendai Nihon bunmei shi* (Tokyo, 1941), pp. 84-86.

the archives of the Ministry of Agriculture were destroyed during the great Kanto earthquake of 1923. In addition, a large quantity of material concerning village political, social and economic life in the early twentieth century appears to have been destroyed by local officials in the immediate postwar era—not, we are told by a Japanese scholar who ought to know, because they contained incriminating evidence, but because they were not written by brush in a fine hand and thus were thought to lack historical value.[17]

Moreover, few landlords, even those who made significant contributions to agricultural development or local government, published diaries or memoirs. For information on their way of life and their attitudes toward the society in which they lived, one must rely on secondary sources. These, however, are limited in scope. Most studies focus on the Tokugawa and early Meiji periods and emphasize the economic activities of landlords rather than their political or cultural interests. Relevant information about landlords in later years, especially after 1920, is very sketchy, partly because the landlords, self-conscious of their position in an era of widespread tenant unrest, were reluctant to discuss their personal lives and partly because contemporary observers of rural affairs were themselves more interested in the new phenomenon of tenant militancy than in the old and familiar landed elite.

For these reasons neither a rigorous statistical analysis of landlords as a whole nor a detailed study of a few representative landlord families is possible. What follows is a fairly general account. Unless otherwise noted, my discussion will be confined to the "main islands" of Japan and will not include Hokkaido, Okinawa, or Japan's colonial possessions.[18] It will be concerned primarily with

17. Furushima Toshio, "Meiji Taishō kyōdo shi kenkyū hō," in *Meiji Taishō kyōdo shi kenkyū hō,* eds., Furushima Toshio et al. (Tokyo, 1970), pp. 25, 27-28.

18. Landlords in Hokkaido, where the scale of farming was larger than on the other main islands of Japan, are discussed in Asada Kyōji, *Nihon shihonshugi to jinushi sei* (Tokyo, 1963). For discussion of landlords and land ownership in Japan's colonial possessions, see by the same author, "Kyūshokuminchi Chōsen ni okeru Nihonjin ōjinushi kaikyū no henbō katei," *Nōgyō sōgō kenkyū* 19:4 (October 1965) and 20:1 (January 1966); "Kyūshokuminchi Taiwan ni okeru Nihonjin ōjinushi

landlords whose holdings consisted solely or principally of rice paddy, throughout the period under discussion the most desirable type of land.[19] Wherever possible, I shall include specific examples and illustrations, but I can present no extended case studies of particular landlords or rural communities. I hope, however, that I will be able to map the basic contours of the forest even if I cannot describe precisely its many trees.

---

kaikyū no sonzai keitai," *Nōgyō sōgō kenkyū* 20:2 (April 1966). Okinawa was not considered an integral part of Japan during most of the period under discussion.

19. In a majority of prefectures more paddy than dry land was tenanted. Within any given prefecture rice-growing regions tended to have the highest percentages of tenanted land. Thus, these landlords may be considered typical. Araki, "Jinushi sei," p. 72. For information on landlords involved in sericulture, see Masanori Nakamura, "The Formation of Money Capital in the Silk Reeling Industry," *Rural Economic Problems* 2 (May 1965): 57–69; Takahashi Kōhachirō and Furushima Toshio, eds., *Yosangyō no hattatsu to jinushi sei* (Tokyo, 1958). For landlords owning forest land, see Fukumoto Kazuo, *Nihon no sanrin ōjinushi* (Tokyo, 1954).

CHAPTER TWO

Landlords and Landlord-Tenant Relations in the Meiji Era

The Meiji Land Settlement

The Meiji land settlement, carried out by the leaders of the Restoration in the years after 1868, brought about what Ronald Dore has described as a stage 1 land reform, comparable to the expropriation of the landed aristocracy in revolutionary France, Eastern Europe after World War I, and India in the 1940s and 1950s.[1] The more than 250 daimyo who had controlled the land and people in their respective domains since the seventeenth century were dispossessed, although with generous compensation. The Meiji government granted farmers private property rights and by 1872 revoked all laws prohibiting the alienation of agricultural land and restricting its use, which had been imposed by the Tokugawa regime. Controls on the occupational mobility of farmers and on their dress, diet and deportment were also lifted. Title deeds were issued to those persons recognized by custom to be in possession of each plot of land. The land tax, generally levied in produce during the Tokugawa period, was converted into an annual money tax of 3 percent of the assessed value of the land, payable to the central govern-

1. Ronald Dore, "Land Reform and Japan's Economic Development," *The Developing Economies* 3 (December 1965): 487–89.

ment by all landowners—with an additional maximum of 1 percent permitted for local taxes.[2]

Although most former daimyo remained wealthy and as members of the House of Peers gained a direct voice in the political system after 1890, they were no longer a landed aristocracy with the power to control local affairs. A few of them, it is true—the Shimazu of Satsuma and the Hosokawa of Kumamoto, for example—were able to get part of their former domains recognized as private holdings. Others invested in tracts of land in Hokkaido, where a large-scale program of agricultural development was begun soon after the Restoration, or acquired holdings of farmland elsewhere.[3] More commonly, however, they invested in forest land, in new industrial enterprises, and perhaps most of all, in banking.[4] Even if part of their income was derived from agriculture, it was generally a small part, overshadowed by their other interests. They no longer exercised political control over the land they owned, and although they were represented in the House of Peers, that body was at no time the center of political power. Unlike England, then, where the landed aristocracy maintained its political influence and by means of the Corn Laws protected the agricultural income on which its power was based until a relatively advanced stage of industrial development, Japan in the decades after the Meiji Restoration was ruled by bureaucrats, the former samurai who had led the Restoration movement and who had been divorced de facto from the land for centuries. Dependent on salaries rather than rents or tithes, they had no personal interest in protecting agricultural wealth and were able to maintain a high level of taxation on agricultural land.[5]

2. Ogura Takekazu, *Tochi rippō no shiteki kōsatsu* (Tokyo, 1951), pp. 99-108; Ono Takeo, *Nōson shi,* vol. 9 of *Gendai Nihon bunmei shi* (Tokyo, 1941), p. 45.

3. Wakukawa Seiyei, "The Japanese Farm Tenancy System," in *Japan's Prospect,* ed. D. G. Haring (Cambridge, Massachusetts, 1946), p. 130.

4. Allan B. Cole, *Japanese Society and Politics: The Impact of Mobility and Social Stratification* (Boston, 1956), p. 16.

5. Dore, "Land Reform and Economic Development," p. 490.

The new tax system, moreover, by eliminating the practice of granting tax reductions when harvests were poor and by requiring the payment of taxes in cash rather than produce, permitted the government to plan its income and expenditure to a degree previously impossible, but essential to the operation of a modern governmental system. The principal source of government revenue until the 1890s, the land tax enabled the new government to solidify its own position and to play an active role in stimulating the industrial development of the nation.

But the daimyo had not been the only landlords in Japan during the Tokugawa period. Standing between them and the actual cultivators of the land in many cases was yet another group with claims on the produce of the soil. Some of these landlords were *gōshi,* the rural samurai who had escaped Hideyoshi's "sword hunt" and remained on the land at the end of the sixteenth century or who were resettled in the countryside by their daimyo after the establishment of Tokugawa hegemony.[6] Others were peasants who had once cultivated large-scale holdings with the labor of *nago,* or serfs, but who, during the eighteenth and early nineteenth centuries, gradually reduced the area of land farmed in this way and leased the greater part of their holdings to their *nago,* commuting labor services into rents in kind.[7]

Probably the most numerous, however, were landlords who acquired title to land by financing reclamation projects or by moneylending. Throughout the Tokugawa period, and especially after the famines which ravaged the country between 1783 and 1788, both the *bakufu* and the daimyo encouraged land reclamation, offering temporary tax relief and other concessions to the men who carried it out. Those supplying the capital for these projects were often wealthy merchants who thereby gained title to the newly opened land, while

6. Ronald Dore, *Land Reform in Japan* (London, 1959), p. 13.

7. Thomas C. Smith, *The Agrarian Origins of Modern Japan* (New York, 1966), pp. 124–39; by the same author, "The Japanese Village in the Seventeenth Century," *The Journal of Economic History* 12 (Winter 1952): 10–15.

the peasants who cultivated it and who, in most cases, had actually done the work involved in reclamation, became their tenants.[8]

Although the ban on the alienation of land imposed by the Tokugawa regime remained in effect until the Restoration, the mortgaging of land was permitted after 1720. Lending money or rice to hard-pressed farmers was often the first step in acquiring possession of their land. Those who gained control of land in this way might be town merchants, members of the emerging class of rural capitalists, or prosperous farmers. An example of the latter were the Itō of Niigata Prefecture, who after the Restoration became one of the largest landowning families in Japan. Originally small-scale culti-vators, they lived in Somi, a way-station along the Shinano River which was visited each year by boats carrying rice to the storehouses in Niigata harbor. By extending credit to the boatmen, the Itō amassed their original capital. Then they made loans to farmers in the area, many of whom suffered periodic losses from flood damage, accepting mortgages on their land as security. By foreclosures they were able to acquire some 20 *chō* of land by 1868.[9] When customary ownership of land was transferred in this way, the new owner could, of course, engage in farming himself. More commonly, however, the former owner became his tenant, paying not only the taxes on the land but also an additional portion of the harvest as rent.

8. Saitō Eiichi, "Jinushi no zaisan kōsei ni tsuite," part 1, *Shakai seisaku jihō,* No. 156 (September 1933), p. 64; Wagatsuma Tōsaku, "Jinushi seido to buraku seido no kankei," *Teikoku nōkai hō* 33 (May 1943): 2; Johannes Hirschmeier, *Entrepreneurship in Meiji Japan* (Cambridge, Massachusetts, 1964), p. 75.

9. Kubo Yasuo, Niigata Prefecture Agricultural Construction Office, personal interview, 10 August 1967. For other examples see Kondō Yasuo, *Mura no kōzō* (Tokyo, 1955), pp. 265-66. Hirschmeier, *Entrepreneurship,* pp. 78, 85. In some domains officials tried to prevent mortgage foreclosures—for example, by declaring that any merchant who acquired land already under cultivation would have to pay twice the normal burden of taxes. Oikawa Shirō, ed., *Yamagata ken nōchi kaikaku shi* (Yamagata, 1953), p. 8. Some farmers, however, hard-pressed for immediate cash, agreed to continue paying all taxes due on the parcels of land they sold from the crops raised on their remaining holding. The government was therefore unaware that a transfer of ownership occurred. Kamagata Isao, *Yamagata ken inasaku shi* (Tokyo, 1953), pp. 392-93.

It has been estimated that roughly 27 percent of all arable land was controlled by these landlords at the time of the Restoration.[10] By 1883, the figure had risen to 36 percent. Regional differences in the extent of tenanted land at this later date were pronounced, and it is probably not inaccurate to assume that, despite the lapse of time, roughly the same differences prevailed in 1868. Tenancy was most common in the economically advanced regions of the country and least common in relatively undeveloped regions. For example, in the Kinki region, which included Osaka, Kyoto and a number of other commercial centers, tenanted land accounted for 40.2 percent of all arable land. In contrast, only 25.1 percent of the land in the six prefectures of the Tohoku, the most backward region of the country, was tenanted.[11]

These differences are in accord with the generally accepted idea that the development of tenancy during the Tokugawa period was largely the result of the penetration of a money economy into the countryside and the growth of commercial farming. It was, for example, the rise in the cost of agricultural production and the shortage of farm labor induced by expanded commercial activity in

10. Furushima Toshio, ed., *Nihon jinushi sei shi kenkyū* (Tokyo, 1958), p. 331. This figure includes Hokkaido.

11. Ibid., p. 332. The Kinki consists of Osaka, Kyoto, Shiga, Hyogo, Nara, Wakayama and Mie Prefectures. The Tohoku consists of Aomori, Iwate, Miyagi, Akita, Yamagata and Fukushima Prefectures. In many discussions of landlords and landlord-tenant relations, however, Okayama and Kagawa Prefectures are treated as part of the Kinki, and Tochigi, Ibaraki and Niigata Prefectures are treated as part of the Tohoku. For example, see Nōchi kaikaku kiroku iinkai, ed., *Nōchi kaikaku tenmatsu gaiyō* (Tokyo, 1951), p. 766 (Table 1B). Concerning regional differences in the extent of tenanted land in early Meiji, one scholar observes that tenancy generally was more pronounced in areas formerly under the direct control of the Tokugawa *bakufu* than in the domains of daimyo in the same region. In prefectures with high percentages of tenancy in the 1880s, the percentage was yet higher in former *bakufu* territories; even in prefectures with low percentages of tenancy there was a noticeably higher percentage of tenancy in districts previously under *bakufu* control. Niwa Kunio, *Keisei ki no Meiji jinushi sei* (Tokyo, 1964), pp. 21-22. Niwa attributes the high incidence of tenancy in *bakufu* territories to the "weakness of feudal rule" within them, which facilitated the development of commercial agriculture and rural industry (pp. 13-14). One might add that the Tokugawa house had chosen to govern these territories directly in the first place because of their strategic locations; whether Tokugawa rule was weak or strong, they were likely centers of economic development.

the latter part of the Tokugawa period which led many large-scale cultivators to abandon farming and lease out most of their land to former *nago*; the accumulation of wealth among merchants, successful farmers, or rural manufacturers which enabled them to finance land reclamation projects and engage in moneylending; and the accumulation of debts among small cultivators as they became involved in the money economy which forced them to mortgage or pawn their land.[12] Because these developments were more pronounced in regions like the Kinki, more land came under the control of landlords there. In the Tohoku these developments were not entirely absent, but they were much less marked. Thus, at the end of the Tokugawa period in the Tohoku one still finds examples of the use of *nago* in large-scale farming.[13]

How many landlords of the types discussed above there were throughout Japan at the time of the Restoration is, of course, not known. What is clear, however, is that they, unlike the daimyo, were not eliminated by the Meiji land settlement. Indeed, they benefited handsomely from it.

First, they gained clear title to their land. The deeds which the government began issuing in 1871 were given to those persons customarily recognized as landowners, but in a society in which there had been no clear conception of private property rights in the past and where local practices and attitudes regarding both land ownership and tenancy had varied widely, the determination of ownership was no easy matter. In many parts of the country, for example, especially where the ban on the alienation of land had been rigorously enforced, the tenant and not the landlord had paid the land tax and had been listed in official registers as the holder of the land.[14] Unaware of local differences and impatient to get the new tax system under way, however, the government generally gave

12. Smith, *Agrarian Origins*, pp. 121–23; Dore, *Land Reform*, pp. 12–13.
13. Ibid., pp. 13–14, 42. Holdings of 10 *chō* or more remained numerous in the Tohoku even though only a relatively small proportion of the land was tenanted. See Araki Moriaki, "Jinushi sei no tenkai," in *Iwanami kōza Nihon rekishi* 16 (Tokyo, 1962): 82 (Table 2-20).
14. Ogura, *Tochi rippō*, p. 110.

17

deeds to anyone receiving rents or holding mortgages.[15] Where there were conflicting claims to the land, the richer and more powerful claimant—the landlord—usually received the deed.[16] Two forms of permanent tenancy which had existed during the Tokugawa period, and of which the government was apparently oblivious, failed to gain legal recognition, and many cultivators became ordinary tenants at will of their landlords. The government did recognize a third form of permanent tenancy but urged that it be eliminated, either by the landlord buying out the tenant's right, by the tenant buying the land, or by the division of the land between landlord and tenant. Here again, the landlord, as the more powerful party, was usually able to gain unrestricted title to the land.[17]

Second, the profits landlords made from leasing land increased. Although the new tax system demanded the payment of taxes in cash, it did not call for any change in the nature of rents. As in the past they were levied in kind, generally in rice, at a fixed volume per unit area which averaged out to over half the crop.[18] At first the taxes landlords and other landowners paid were roughly equivalent to those imposed during the Tokugawa period, although the tax burden increased in some areas of the country and decreased in others. In 1878, in response to widespread protests, primarily from landowners whose taxes had increased, the tax rate was reduced to 2.5 percent of the assessed value of land. Then in 1884 the government abandoned its original plan to revise legal land values, the basis of the tax, every five years.[19] Since the tax was now fixed, the gradual rise in rice prices thereafter caused a progressive reduction

15. Ono Takeo, "Meiji keizai shi yori mitaru kosaku undō bokkō no genryū," *Sangyō kumiai,* No. 261 (1927), pp. 3-4.

16. Dore, *Land Reform,* p. 16; Ogura, *Tochi rippō,* p. 121.

17. Ibid., pp. 110-11. For an excellent discussion of the problems facing the government in carrying out the tax reform see Niwa, *Meiji jinushi sei,* pp. 126-59.

18. Ono, *Nōson shi,* p. 82; Ogura, *Tochi rippō,* pp. 109, 137-38. For example, rent might be set at 1 *koku* per *tan* where yields normally were 2 *koku* per *tan.* Only in remote regions of the country was sharecropping (*kariwake kosaku*) practiced. One *koku* of rice equals roughly five bushels.

19. Ibid., p. 127.

in its real value. Landlords received the same volume of rice as rents, but had to devote a smaller proportion of the proceeds from its sale to tax payments.[20]

Third, the land settlement gave landlords the opportunity to acquire more land. As noted previously, all restrictions on the alienation of land were removed. More important, however, was the effect of the new land tax on small owner-cultivators, especially during the depression of the early 1880s. Lacking savings and unable to gain enough money from the sale of their crops to cover taxes and living expenses, many were forced into debt and lost part of their land to moneylenders, merchants, or already established landlords.[21] Thus, the extent of tenanted land rose from 36 percent of all arable land in 1883 to 45 percent in 1908.[22]

The land settlement also induced changes in landlord-tenant relations. Some of these were relatively minor. During the Tokugawa period, for example, the levees between paddy fields were not subject to taxes or rents even though crops were sometimes grown upon them. Under the Meiji tax system, however, if anything was cultivated on the levees, land taxes were imposed, and some landlords now began charging rents on the levees as well as on the fields themselves.[23] But changes of greater importance stemmed from the elimination of direct governmental supervision of tenancy.

In some parts of the country during the Tokugawa period the level of rents which landlords could charge was fixed by the domain government, a policy designed to protect small cultivators and, by extension, the tax revenues which they produced. With the land settlement, however, all forms of official rent control were abandoned. When asked in 1875 what steps it recommended for dealing with landlords who were now raising rents, the Home Ministry replied that under the new system of private land ownership rent

20. Ono, *Nōson shi*, p. 47.
21. Ibid., pp. 58–59; Saitō, "Zaisan kōsei,," pp. 66–67.
22. Dore, *Land Reform*, p. 19. Dore states that tenanted land accounted for 37 percent of all arable land in 1883, not 36 percent.
23. Ogura, *Tochi rippō*, p. 139.

levels were the sole concern of landlords and their tenants and not a matter requiring action by the government.[24]

Similarly, rent arrears were often handled by officials during the Tokugawa period. In what later became Tottori Prefecture, a landlord was not allowed to evict a tenant who failed to pay his rent on time. Instead, he was required to report the matter to the village headman who then confiscated the tenant's crop and, after deducting taxes, gave the landlord his share. The tenant, however, was allowed to remain as cultivator of the land. But after the Restoration rent arrears, like rent levels, became a private matter. No longer restrained by official efforts to protect cultivators, landlords sometimes used eviction, or the threat of eviction, as a means of dealing with unpaid rents.[25] As property owners, the Home Ministry observed, they were now free to do whatever they wished with their land.[26]

As noted previously, tenant farmers, and not their landlords, were responsible for paying land taxes in many parts of the country during the Tokugawa period. Listed as landholders in official registers, they received a certain amount of advice and protection directly from the government. If the time and place of paying taxes were changed, they were so informed. If harvests were poor, the official in charge of collecting local taxes told them, not their landlords, how much the tax payments would be reduced.[27]

After the Restoration this form of governmental supervision was also eliminated, and all tenants paid both the landlord's and the government's share of the crop as rent. Having made landowners responsible for taxes, the new regime had no reason to advise or protect tenant farmers. Its concern now focused on protecting landowners and assuring their ability to pay taxes, a concern which involved, among other things, promoting the ability of landlords to

24. Ibid.
25. Ono, *Nōson shi,* pp. 80–81; for examples of other steps taken by landlords to collect overdue rents, see Ogura, *Tochi rippō,* pp. 144–47.
26. Ibid., p. 139.
27. Ono, *Nōson shi,* pp. 22–23; Kamagata, *Inasaku shi,* p. 384.

collect rents. Rejecting the idea of a special tenancy law to accomplish this end, the government relied instead on the Constitution and the Civil Code. According to Article 27 of the Constitution, the rights of property of Japanese subjects were to be inviolable. Although permanent tenancy was recognized in the Civil Code as a property right (*bukken*), a limit of fifty years was placed on its duration. Ordinary tenancy, by far the more common form,[28] was defined in the Code as an obligation (*saiken*), not as a property right. Landlords could cancel tenancy agreements at any time and were not required by law to compensate tenants for any improvements they had made on the land.[29]

The Meiji land settlement, then, upset the previous distribution of power between landlords and tenants. Their property rights almost totally unrestricted, landlords were permitted by law to deal with tenants in any way they chose. Unprotected and to a great extent ignored by the government,[30] tenants were more vulnerable to exploitation than ever before.

The land settlement did not gain immediate acceptance in the Japanese countryside. In some parts of the country the tax reform brought about an increase in the burden of land taxes, leading to demands by local landowners that the government reduce either the assessed value of their land or the tax rate.[31] Some landowners complained that there was insufficient currency in circulation, making it impossible to pay taxes in money rather than in kind.[32] Farmers

28. Ordinary tenancy accounted for roughly 99 percent of all tenanted land by the turn of the century. Dore, *Land Reform,* p. 64.

29. Ono, "Kosaku undō bokkō no genryū," pp. 3-4; Ogura, *Tochi rippō,* pp. 180-82, 221.

30. And by the government's critics as well. Not until the early 1900s, well after their "discovery" of poverty among urban workers, did Japanese intellectuals and social reformers begin in a serious way to call attention to the problems tenant farmers faced. As David Mitrany observes about Europe, so too in Japan there was no Dickens of the village poor. *Marx Against the Peasant* (Chapel Hill, 1951), p. 123.

31. Ono, *Nōson shi,* pp. 48, 66-67. Ono observes that in a few villages in Owari (Aichi Prefecture) the new land tax imposed ten times the burden of the old. Increases were usually considerably less.

32. Ono Takeo, *Meiji zenki tochi seido shiron* (Tokyo, 1948), p. 196.

protested, too, that village common land, important to them as a source of fuel and fodder, was being unfairly claimed by the state as government land or by individuals as private property.[33]

Tenant farmers, especially those owning some land of their own, were apt to join with other villagers in protests over tax levels, shortages of currency, or loss of common land. In addition, some tenants initiated protests of their own, against the land settlement in general and against their landlords. Their grievances centered on two major issues: rights to land and rents.

Tenant protests over the loss of customarily recognized permanent tenancy rights were most common in the early Meiji era,[34] but farmers who had pawned or mortgaged the land they cultivated lodged protests, too, when title deeds were given to their creditors rather than to them. In those parts of the country where the tax reform brought about a decrease in the burden of land taxes, tenants demanded that rents, too, be lowered. Furthermore, when the government reduced the nationwide land tax rate from 3 percent to 2.5 percent in 1878, tenants in many villages demanded corresponding rent reductions from their landlords.[35]

In only a minority of cases were tenants successful in pressing their demands. Defeat was far more common, especially if the dispute was taken to court. In Kochi Prefecture, for example, a group of tenants with permanent tenancy rights demanded rent reductions when the land tax rate was reduced in 1878. Their landlords refused, so they filed a suit, which they promptly lost. Two of the tenants appealed the decision to a higher court, arguing that as permanent tenants they had a vested interest (*kitokuken*) in the land they cultivated and that as payers of rent they actually bore the burden of the land tax. Initially the court decided that landlords and tenants should benefit equally from the tax reduction and ordered that rents be reduced accordingly. The landlords appealed the decision, however, and the court reversed itself, deciding that landlords alone,

33. Ibid., pp. 193-94, 291-92.
34. Ibid., pp. 287-88.
35. Ibid., pp. 193-94, 196-97, 290-94.

as property owners and legal taxpayers, were entitled to the full benefit of the tax reduction.[36]

After 1884, when the government announced that land values would not be reassessed every five years as originally planned, rural protests over the land tax declined in number. Tenant protests, too, subsided in the late 1880s. Not until the post-World War I era did tenancy disputes again become widespread.

Landlord-Tenant Relations in the Meiji Era

An underlying cause of tenancy disputes in the 1870s and 1880s had been the government's ignorance of the diverse types of tenancy that had evolved throughout the country during the preceding centuries of decentralized rule. No comprehensive study of tenancy practices was carried out in advance of the land settlement. Instead, prefectural officials, who rarely knew much about farming, were ordered to issue title deeds and assess land values as quickly as possible. In carrying out their charge, they paid little heed to the varieties of tenancy or to the nuances of landlord-tenant relations within their jurisdictions. The result was protest by tenants over the loss of rights long sanctioned by local custom.

When the first nationwide survey of tenancy practices was carried out in 1885, roughly a decade after completion of the land settlement, it revealed that over twenty different types of tenancy had existed at the time of the Restoration.[37] The most common of these types, found throughout the country, were as follows:

1. Permanent tenancy (*eikosaku*), in which tenants possessed "perpetual" cultivating rights, acquired by their labor in reclaiming the land or by virtue of farming the same plot for a specified period of time (usually twenty years or more). Permanent tenants could not be dislodged from the land they cultivated, or could only be

36. Ibid., pp. 206, 289, 295–96.
37. The survey itself was lost in the 1923 Kanto earthquake, but a summary of its findings still exists, and some details and examples appear in secondary sources published before 1923. The different types of tenancy uncovered by the survey are analyzed in Ono, *Meiji zenki tochi seido shiron,* pp. 223–35, on which the following discussion is based.

dislodged for certain specific reasons such as the landlord's need to cultivate the land himself. In a sense, owing to their strong cultivating rights, permanent tenants shared "ownership" of the land with their landlords. As a further reflection of their status, they generally paid lower rents than did other kinds of tenants.

2. Direct tenancy (*jikikosaku*), in which a landholder put his land in pawn but remained on it as a tenant, paying rent to the lender. The balance left after taxes and other charges had been deducted from the rent constituted the interest payment on the loan. The principal was due in three years or so, at which time the borrower regained possession of the land. Direct tenancy was a product of the ban on the alienation of land in force during the Tokugawa period, and because a direct tenant could eventually redeem his land, he was recognized to possess stronger cultivating rights than an ordinary tenant who had never owned the land he farmed.

3. "Separate" tenancy (*betsu kosaku*), in which pawned land was tenanted by someone other than the original holder. As in direct tenancy, the rent paid by the tenant was used to pay land taxes and interest to the moneylender. Typically, the original holder used the money he received to establish himself in an occupation other than farming. If he repaid the loan, he regained possession of the land. Like direct tenancy, separate tenancy was a product of the ban on the alienation of land.

4. Caretaker tenancy (*yamori kosaku*), in which an individual with land in a village other than his own entrusted its management to someone living in that village. The caretaker farmed part of the land himself, retaining all the crops he raised. He let the rest to tenants and himself collected their rents. After paying taxes, he sent the remaining rent to the landholder. This form of tenancy arose not only because of the difficulty of supervising distant landholdings, but also because the village, not the individual, was the basic unit of taxation during the Tokugawa period. If an individual held land in another village, it was convenient—and in some regions, essential—to have a village resident assume responsibility for tax payments.

5. Contract tenancy (*ukeoi kosaku*), in which an individual was designated manager of tenanted land, with full responsibility for collecting rents and paying taxes. The manager also paid the land-holder a fixed volume of the rents received, keeping the remainder for himself as compensation for his duties. Like caretaker tenancy, contract tenancy was resorted to when someone acquired land in another village.

6. Ordinary tenancy (*futsū kosaku, tsūjō kosaku*), in which a landholder himself let land to tenants, the latter having no special relationship to him or to the land they farmed. If tenants were able to continue cultivating the land long enough, they might eventually acquire permanent tenancy rights.[38]

Less common types of tenancy, found only in a few prefectures at most, included:

1. Deposit tenancy (*shikikin kosaku*), in which tenants paid land-lords several years' rent in advance and then began cultivating their land. Deposit tenancy existed in regions where there was intense competition among tenants for available land.

2. Sharecropping (*kariwake kosaku*), in which tenants paid land-lords a fixed percentage, not a fixed volume, of their crops.

3. Subtenancy (*mago kosaku, mata kosaku*), in which tenants sublet their land to others.

4. Joint tenancy (*renmei kosaku*), in which several tenants culti-vated the same plot(s) of land.

5. Service tenancy (*tsutome kosaku*), in which tenants paid their landlord in labor rather than in crops.

6. Dependent tenancy (*kadowake kosaku, kehō kosaku, uchi kosaku, nago kosaku*), in which household servants or other indi-viduals related in some way to the landholder cultivated small plots of his land, providing labor or rent in return.

7. Credit tenancy (*shiire kosaku*), in which landlords provided tenants with seeds and fertilizer, the cost of which was added to

---

38. Ono notes that *myōden kosaku,* defined in some sources as a form of permanent tenancy, was actually equivalent to ordinary tenancy in the early Meiji era. It could lead, however, to permanent tenancy. Ibid., pp. 230, 242–43.

their rents. A variant form was *kabu kosaku,* in which the landlord also supplied tenants with houses and farm tools.

8. Cash tenancy (*kanekosaku*), in which tenants paid their rents in cash rather than in crops.

With the land settlement, many of the above types of tenancy began to disappear, and ordinary tenancy, already widespread at the time of the Restoration, became almost universal. Acting on the principle of "one plot, one owner," government officials urged the elimination of all cases of "shared ownership," permanent tenancy being the prime example. In addition, with the lifting of the ban on the alienation of land, there no longer was any necessity for direct (or separate) tenancy. Like the majority of permanent tenants, many direct tenants, even those about to redeem their land, became ordinary tenants as creditors acquired full ownership of pawned land. Because individual landowners were now the basic unit of taxation, one could assume direct control of land in other villages. Only landlords with extensive holdings in a large number of villages continued to rely on caretaker or contract tenancy. Finally, with the rise in rice prices after the depression of the early 1880s, it became advantageous for landlords to receive rice rather than labor services as rent. Only in remote parts of the country did service and dependent tenancy survive.[39]

Despite the reduction in the number of different types of tenancy, landlord-tenant relations remained fairly complex. In most cases, tenants rented the land they cultivated not from one but from several landlords. For example, Koyama Mitsugu of Nango village, Miyagi Prefecture, cultivated a total of 1.6 *chō* of paddy which he rented in separate parcels from five different landlords.[40] In a village in Yamagata Prefecture, most tenants had three or four landlords, and a few had eight or nine.[41] In part, this was the product of an

---

39. Ibid., pp. 235-39.
40. Sunaga Shigemitsu, ed., *Kindai Nihon no jinushi to nōmin* (Tokyo, 1966), p. 321.
41. Nasu Shiroshi, *Shōnai tadokoro no nōgyō nōson oyobi seikatsu* (Tokyo, 1941), pp. 48-49.

"unwritten law" of tenant survival: since tenants possessed few, if any, rights, they sought to spread the risks they faced of rent increases or eviction by avoiding undue reliance on a single landlord.[42] It was also caused, however, by the fragmented nature of landholdings. As shown previously in Table 2, the vast majority of landlords owned 5 *chō* of land or less. Most commonly, their holdings consisted of a number of tiny parcels, each no more than a few *tan* in area, acquired here and there in their own or neighboring villages at different times. Only larger landlords, or the owners of tracts of reclaimed land, were likely to own enough land in one location to provide all the land a tenant needed to cultivate.[43]

Moreover, just as tenants had several landlords, landlords usually had several tenants. Indeed, some very large landlords had hundreds of tenants, and a few had over one thousand. The tenants of any given landlord, large or small, were likely to form a heterogeneous group. In the early Meiji era, some might have permanent cultivating rights while others were ordinary tenants and still others performed labor services in exchange for land. Even if all the tenants of a landlord were ordinary tenants—increasingly the case after the land settlement—they were still likely to differ markedly from one another. Some might be completely landless while others owned land of their own.[44] Or some might be part-time farmers, supplementing their income as tenants with wages from non-agricultural employment, while others relied solely on farming for their livelihoods.

As an illustration of the heterogeneity of a landlord's tenants, consider the case of the Hirose family, substantial landlords in

42. Kubo Yasuo, personal interview; Fukutake Tadashi, *Japanese Rural Society* (London, 1967), p. 13.
43. How much land a tenant required depended, among other things, on the region in which he lived: more land was needed in the single-crop zone of northeastern Japan than in the multiple-crop zones of the southwest. Fukutake observes that half a hectare (roughly 5 *tan*) was the bare minimum. Ibid., p. 7.
44. Some might even be tenant-landlords. That is, if an individual owned land too distant from his place of residence he might lease it to tenants and then rent land nearby for his own use. Farmers usually cultivated scattered parcels of land, but only rarely was the land located in more than two villages. In fact, farming

Nakakoma *gun,* a rice-growing region in Yamanashi Prefecture.[45] In the early 1890s, the Hirose owned roughly 37 *chō* in Tōda, the village in which they lived, and a total of 25 additional *chō* in nine neighboring villages. Their land in Tōda was cultivated by ninety-three tenants, thirty-two of whom appear to have owned no land at all. The sixty-one tenants who also owned land fell into three distinct categories: 1) those who owned less than 3 *tan* and tenanted less than 5 *tan* for total holdings of less than 8 *tan,* 2) those who cultivated 1 *chō* or more and who owned at least as much land as they tenanted, and 3) those who cultivated 1 *chō* or more but who owned much less land than they tenanted. Tenants in the first category could not support their families by farming alone (unless they rented land from someone else) and needed other employment. Tenants in both the second and third categories could make a living from farming, but their statuses were by no means identical. Those in the second category were likely to think of themselves as owner-cultivators who also leased land, while those in the third category were likely to think of themselves as tenants who also owned some land. The latter were more dependent on the Hirose than the former, as were the thirty-two landless tenants.

The Hirose, like virtually all landlords in the Meiji era, made individual tenancy agreements with each of their tenants. Most such agreements were oral (although the landlord might keep a record of them), but written contracts, signed by the tenant and one or two guarantors, were employed in some cases, especially by landlords with extensive holdings and in villages where tenancy disputes had occurred in the aftermath of the land settlement.[46] Some agreements—the Hirose's, for example—were made annually, but most were for a period of three to five years.[47] Their key provision was the

---

was usually confined to the hamlet in which the individual lived. Tōbata Seiichi, *Nōchi o meguru jinushi to nōmin* (Tokyo, 1947), pp. 25–27.

45. Nagahara Keiji et al., *Nihon jinushi sei no kōsei to dankai* (Tokyo, 1972), pp. 323–25, 340. This book contains excellent case studies of four Yamanashi landlords.

46. Ono, *Meiji zenki tochi seido shiron,* pp. 277–80.

47. Ibid., pp. 240–50. Ono notes a trend toward short, fixed terms of tenancy in the early Meiji period.

volume of rent due each year. On paddy, rents were levied either in hulled or unhulled rice; rents generally were charged on the main rice crop alone, enabling tenants in regions where double-cropping was possible to retain for themselves—to consume or to market— any secondary crops they raised.[48] As noted previously, except in cases of permanent tenancy, landlords had the right to cancel tenancy agreements at any time.

In these purely economic and legal terms, the status of tenants in the late nineteenth century was precarious indeed. Cultivating small plots of land to begin with, they paid roughly half the crops they raised as rent. Possessing few if any rights, they had no legal recourse in the face of harsh or arbitrary treatment. But landlord-tenant relations at this time went well beyond the simple exchange of parcels of land for rent, and law played far less of a role in governing the behavior of both landlords and tenants than did custom. Tenants might protest what they considered unfair treatment, but they continued to accept the hierarchical structure of power in the countryside and their own subordinate position.

In part this was because the "expressive" aspects of the relationship between landlords and tenants helped "in allaying hostility and in softening the blow . . . of economic hardship."[49] Most landlords in the Meiji era appear to have resided in the countryside, fairly close to the land they owned.[50] They saw their tenants often, sometimes daily, and knew them and members of their families by name. Throughout the country kinship terms were applied to tenancy relations. The landlord was the *oyakata* (father); his own farming,

48. Rents on paddy which could be double-cropped usually were somewhat higher than on paddy which could produce only a single rice crop (see Table 3, p. 61), but they were not so high as to deprive tenants of the opportunity to profit. In one village, for example, tenants paid 1.6 *koku* of rice per *tan* as rent, almost 60 percent of yield. But on the same land in the winter they could raise, and keep for themselves, 1.55 *koku* per *tan* of wheat or barley; some were also able to harvest a third crop of vegetables before the next rice planting. Kondō, *Mura no kōzō*, p. 427.

49. John W. Bennett and Iwao Ishino, *Paternalism in the Japanese Economy* (Minneapolis, 1963), p. 216.

50. An exception, of course, were those urban merchants who also owned arable land.

oyasaku (cultivation by the father). Tenancy was *kosaku* (cultivation by the child), or where one tenant sublet land from another, *mago-saku* (cultivation by the grandchild).[51] As Dore has observed, these and similar terms did not necessarily imply affection. Rather, they served to associate tenancy with the highly authoritarian Japanese family.[52] Like the family, tenancy was part of the natural and accepted social order. And like family members, landlords and tenants celebrated births and marriages together and helped each other bury their dead. Most landlords provided feasts for their tenants after the harvest, at New Year's, and on other holidays. In some cases, tenants joined landlords in worshipping common ancestors.[53]

But the functional aspects of the landlord-tenant relationship were, I think, of greater importance in sustaining acceptance by tenants of their subordinate position. Although relatively unchecked by law in their dealings with tenants, landlords were not completely free of constraints. Traditional definitions of their role in tenancy relations and village affairs, internalized by landlords as members of rural society, not only restrained them from arbitrarily exercising their power but also induced them to serve their communities in a variety of ways.

All landlords, regardless of the size of their holdings, were expected to protect their tenants from the impact of poor harvests by reducing rents. This traditional practice, although not required by the Civil Code or other legislation,[54] appears to have been observed throughout the country. Significantly, its reverse—the raising of rents when bumper crops were harvested—was virtually unknown.[55]

---

51. Amano Fujio, *Nōson shakai mondai: jinushi to kosakunin* (Tokyo, 1920), p. 5.

52. Dore, *Land Reform*, p. 39.

53. Wagatsuma, "Jinushi seido," p. 6; Amano, *Nōson shakai mondai*, p. 29; Bennett and Ishino, *Paternalism*, pp. 203–4, 216.

54. The Civil Code merely stipulated that if yield on leased land fell below the level of rent, tenants had the right to demand that rent be reduced to the level of yield. Dore, *Land Reform*, p. 65.

55. Ogura, *Tochi rippō*, pp. 141–42. It was understood, of course, that if yield declined because of the tenant's negligence, not as the result of forces beyond his control, no reduction would be necessary.

There were, of course, regional differences in the granting of reductions. In the single-crop zone of northeastern Japan even a small decrease in yield called for a reduced rent. If the harvest was especially poor the landlord and tenant might divide the crop, or the landlord might waive rent altogether. Where multiple-cropping was possible, however, and the opportunity of recouping losses on secondary crops existed, only sizable decreases in the rice harvest merited rent reductions.[56] But all landlords were, to one degree or another, involved in sharing the risks of farming with their tenants. And in the Meiji era the risks were considerable. Crop failures could be caused by early frosts in the northeast, late summer typhoons in the southwest, and everywhere by floods, droughts, and insect damage.

Not surprisingly, the recurring need to grant rent reductions motivated many landlords to promote agricultural improvements—a subject to be discussed later. But the practice also had an impact on tenants, most basically by helping to justify to them the high rents they paid: if (or more accurately, when) disaster struck they would be cared for. Tenants apparently were willing to pay very high rents indeed for this protection. In Yamagata Prefecture, for example, it was said that "if you must be a tenant, be a tenant of the Homma,"[57] the largest landowning family in Japan with a holding in the late nineteenth century of over 1,500 *chō*. Homma land was located in the Shōnai plain, part of the northeastern single-crop zone; although high yields of rice were possible in good years, crop failures were not unusual. In the 1890s rents on Homma land amounted to fully 75 percent of the crop, but their generous rent reduction policies, which guaranteed tenants a livelihood no matter what happened to the harvest, made them desirable landlords nonetheless.[58]

In addition to rent reductions, landlords also loaned money to

56. Wolf I. Ladejinsky, "Landlord vs. Tenant in Japan," *Foreign Agriculture* 11 (June 1947): 84; J.W. Robertson Scott, *The Foundations of Japan* (London, 1922), p. 187; Dore, *Land Reform*, pp. 36, 44.
57. Kamagata, *Inasaku shi*, p. 401.
58. Ibid., p. 400. The large parcels of land tenants could obtain from the Homma were a further advantage.

their tenants—sometimes, though not always, at lower than prevailing interest rates[59]—and helped them acquire tools, seeds and fertilizer from town merchants.[60] Larger landlords were expected to provide tenants (or their wives and children) with additional employment in their households or on their own farms. Indeed, there is evidence to suggest that some landlords consciously created employment opportunities for tenants, setting up home industries such as silk-reeling or rope-making to provide off-season work, hiring more household servants than they actually needed, or scheduling repairs or additions to their homes when economic conditions were poor.[61]

Landlords almost always benefited from these activities, of course: they earned interest on their loans, made profits from their home industries, or simply lived more comfortably. But their tenants, and the villages in which they lived, benefited too. In the absence of other off-season work or of government-sponsored public works projects, and at a time when local banks and rural credit associations were only beginning to be organized, tenants were less apt to resent their landlords' wealth than to be thankful for it. It was, after all, a significant factor in their survival from year to year.[62]

A further service which landlords provided was village leadership. Some landlords eschewed local political office, preferring to exert their influence behind the scenes, but most played an active role, serving in such posts as village mayor or treasurer or as members of the village assembly.[63] They won appointment, and later, election, to these positions not simply because of their superior ascriptive status, but also because of their ability to perform tasks the com-

59. Wagatsuma, "Jinushi seido," p. 6.
60. Social Science Research Institute, *The Power Structure in a Rural Community: the Case of Mutsuzawa Mura* (Tokyo, 1960), pp. 2–4.
61. Sunaga, *Kindai Nihon no jinushi to nōmin,* pp. 202–3; Bennett and Ishino, *Paternalism,* pp. 217–18.
62. In England, too, the wealth of landlords was a significant factor in local prosperity. See G. E. Mingay, *English Landed Society in the Eighteenth Century* (London, 1963), pp. 150–62.
63. William J. Chambliss, *Chiaraijima Village: Land Tenure, Taxation, and Local Trade 1818–1884* (Tucson, 1965), pp. 38, 72–74; Social Science Research Institute, *Power Structure,* pp. 23–24.

munity valued. Chief among these was defending the community's interests in dealings with the government and with other villages, a task for which landlords were particularly qualified.

Most landlords in the Meiji era were well-educated. And, as Thomas Smith has observed, [64] their education was not entirely practical. Since the early 1800s landlords and other wealthy farmers had hired tutors to teach their sons philosophy, calligraphy, and martial skills. They not only kept accounts, but wrote poetry and essays on morality. In addition, they had personal contacts in nearby towns and villages, acquired by means of marriage and commercial activity. As men of property and, after 1890, as voters who formed a substantial portion of the national electorate,[65] they merited considerate treatment by bureaucrats and party politicians. As a result they were far better able than other farmers, most of whom were illiterate, to understand the world outside the village and to negotiate with outsiders on the village's behalf—for lower land value assessments at the time of the tax reform and, later, for lower taxes; for new roads and other improvements in transportation which facilitated the commercial sale of crops; or for favorable settlements in local irrigation disputes which guaranteed the community the water it needed to grow rice.[66]

Nor was the landlords' leadership of their villages confined to politics. Many also worked to improve the social and cultural life of their communities. Education provides a case in point. Landlords not only contributed funds for the construction of local schools,[67] but also provided scholarships to enable bright village youths from

64. Smith, *Agrarian Origins* (New York, 1966), pp. 177-79.
65. The franchise in national elections was granted in 1889 to males over 25 years of age who paid 15 yen or more in direct national taxes. Of a total electorate of 453,474 men, only 13,491 qualified to vote on the basis of income tax payments; the vast majority, some 97 percent of the total, were landowners who qualified on the basis of land tax payments. Araki, "Jinushi sei," pp. 98-99.
66. Ono, *Nōson shi,* pp. 66-67; Denda Isao, "Kokuminshugi shisō to nōhonshugi shisō," in *Meiji zenhan ki no nashonarizumu,* ed. Sakata Yoshio (Tokyo, 1958), pp. 277-81; Ogura, *Tochi rippō,* pp. 207-8; Baba Akira, personal interview, 28 May 1967.
67. Dore, "Land Reform and Japan's Economic Development," pp. 492-93. Although the central government established the universal education system, local governments were expected to bear a major share of its costs.

poor families to attend high school and university. Their largesse was not, as the skeptic might argue, merely a clever way of ridding the community of its ablest, and potentially most troublesome, members. Rather, in many cases, students who received such aid were required to work for the village for a few years once their education was complete, putting what they had learned—about farming, medicine, or accounting—to use in the community.[68]

In these and other ways, landlords served as the protectors and benefactors of their tenants and of the villages in which they lived. Of course, not all landlords were equally active in performing the role expected of them, but on the whole they appear to have done enough to justify their elite status: there was a rough parity between the functions they performed and the rewards they received. In addition, both the expressive and functional aspects of the landlord-tenant relationship militated against the development of tenant class consciousness. The vertical ties between landlords and tenants were stronger in most cases than the horizontal ties among tenants themselves,[69] a condition to which the various economic and attitudinal differences among tenants contributed.

By the Taishō era, however, the situation had changed dramatically. In part, the upsurge in landlord-tenant conflict in the 1920s was caused by changes in the attitudes of tenants over which landlords had little or no control—the influence, for example, of universal elementary education in undermining tenant acceptance of traditional status distinctions. But it was also due to the actions of landlords themselves: to the unforeseen consequences of their efforts to promote their own economic interests and to their growing failure to perform the very functions that had justified their elite status in the past—subjects discussed in the next two chapters.

68. See, for example, Inoue Yūichi, "Jinushi to seinen to no rensa," *Teikoku nōkai hō* 2 (March 1912): 20–22; Tōbata, *Nōchi o meguru,* p. 71. Kubo Yasuo suggests that for some landlords aiding bright village youth and demanding that they return to the village was a necessity, since the landlords themselves, owing to generations of intermarriage, had few bright offspring able to manage family and community affairs. Personal interview, 10 August 1967.

69. Bennett and Ishino, *Paternalism,* p. 56. The fewer landlords a tenant had, the stronger these vertical ties.

CHAPTER THREE

Landlords and Agriculture

The Rice Stubble Riot of 1880

Since at least the mid-Tokugawa period, the Chikugo region of
Kyushu (which became Fukuoka Prefecture after the Restoration)
had been plagued by insect damage to its rice crops.[1] In the 1760s
some areas reported no rice harvest at all. Damage was more widespread in the early 1800s, prompting domain officials to open
emergency granaries and cancel taxes.

Local farmers realized there was some sort of connection between
the damage to their crops and the presence of large numbers of
pearl moths, but they knew of no way to eliminate the insects themselves. Instead they relied on the protective deities of their communities. Each year one of the villages in the afflicted area would
stage a festival of dancing and prayer, *sumo* would be performed at
Shinto shrines, and paper charms blessed by the priests would be
placed throughout the rice fields. Damage, however, continued
unabated.

In 1872 Ekita Sohei became the new head of Eguchi village. His
family had provided local leadership for generations, and one may
safely assume that they were landlords.[2] Soon after taking office,

---

1. The following account of the rice stubble riot is from Ono Takeo, *Nōson shi*,
vol. 9 of *Gendai Nihon bunmei shi* (Tokyo, 1941), pp. 259–74.
2. Unfortunately, Ono's account is not clear on this point. He refers to Ekita
merely as an "experienced farmer" (*rōnō*). As Dore observes, however, *rōnō* were

Ekita learned about the scientific study of insects from a farming journal published by the Gakunōsha in Tokyo,[3] and immediately he began his own investigation of the pearl moth. He observed its life cycle from egg to larva to moth, and confirmed that it was the larva, a rice borer, that did the damage. He found, too, by experiments on his own land, that an effective way of controlling the problem was to rake up all the rice stubble left in the fields after the harvest and burn it. In that way the hibernating larvae, which would emerge as pupae and then moths in the spring to continue the cycle, would be destroyed.

Aware that pearl moths afflicted the entire region and that any successful campaign to eliminate them would have to be carried out over a wide area, Ekita then visited prefectural officials and the appropriate bureaus of the central government to urge the dissemination of his findings to all farmers in Fukuoka. This proved to be a mistake. The people of his area wanted nothing to do with a policy imposed on them by outside officials and criticized Ekita for trying to curry favor with the government. Undaunted, he decided to publicize his findings himself, and in 1879 he spoke to a meeting of farmers from the afflicted area. But they could not fully comprehend what he was talking about and voted down his proposal for an areawide campaign of burning. It would require considerable labor, they objected, and they had no assurance it would work.

At that point Ekita obtained funds from the prefectural government to establish an experimental station in the area so that the effectiveness of burning could be demonstrated to skeptical farmers. Apparently this step had the desired effect: the farmers might not understand scientific explanations of insect life, but they could appreciate results. When fields which had been raked and burned showed fewer signs of damage than other fields the following year, opposition began to evaporate.

"for the most part landlords" in the early Meiji era. "Agricultural Improvement in Japan, 1870–1900," *Economic Development and Cultural Change* 9 (October 1960): 80.

3. The Gakunōsha, under the leadership of Tsuda Sen, sought to promote Western farming techniques.

Prefectural officials decided to act right away. Once again a public meeting was held, and for eight days the officials joined Ekita in urging adoption of a regional burning campaign. This time they received a more promising response from the audience. Farmers who had visited the experimental station were willing to consider Ekita's plan seriously; some even spoke up wholeheartedly in favor of it. But there were still those with misgivings, many of whom wondered why the plan could not be adopted gradually and only a few fields burned the first year. When told that half measures would be self-defeating—that the stubble in all fields in the area had to be burned for the plan to succeed—they lapsed into silence.

Finally a vote was called for. Because the chairman of the meeting was a respected local figure who spoke warmly in support of the plan, no one dared oppose it, and it was approved unanimously. But in subsequent weeks, as the time for burning the rice stubble approached, opposition among some local farmers resurfaced. Outsiders had no right to tell them how to manage their land, they complained; they should be resting after the labor of the harvest, not doing additional work. Finally their resentment reached such a point that they rioted, and for roughly a week they roamed the area damaging public property and chanting protests against the government.

Presumably the burning of the rice stubble was carried out after order was restored, and the problem of the pearl moth was solved. One may imagine, too, that improved harvests thereafter helped interest local farmers in scientific approaches to farming. But for a while even the prospect of continued crop failures had not been sufficient to overcome their resistance to change or their resentment of outside interference in their affairs.

Significantly, it had been a member of the local elite who had first discovered a solution to the problem afflicting the area and who had worked for years to win support for it. In so doing, Ekita exemplified the positive role landlords played in promoting agricultural improvements in the Meiji era. It was an activity for which they were well qualified and, for a variety of reasons, highly motivated.

Landlords and Agricultural Improvements

The available data indicate that most landlords in the late nineteenth century did not lease out all, or even a major part, of the land they owned. Instead they farmed a portion of it themselves, using family or hired labor.[4] As a result, they were familiar with local agricultural conditions and apt to be aware of any problems local farmers faced.

In addition, like Ekita, they had access to new ideas about agriculture. Not only could landlords read and understand the many treatises on farming being published by the government and private groups in the late nineteenth century, they could also afford to travel to fairs and exhibitions and to send their sons to the new agricultural schools that were being established in the 1870s and 1880s.[5] As men of wealth, they had both the leisure to experiment with crops or farming techniques and the economic security to assume the risks which experimentation involved. Okada Ryōichirō, a large landlord in Shizuoka Prefecture, spent several years growing sorghum on his own experimental plot in the hope of developing a profitable substitute for cane sugar.[6] A landlord in Gifu Prefecture turned some of his mountain land into a tangerine orchard, knowing he could not expect profits for fifteen years.[7] Others worked on developing new strains of rice, on improving plowing and planting techniques, on determining the optimum amount of fertilizer for

4. Ronald Dore, "The Meiji Landlord: Good or Bad?," *Journal of Asian Studies* 18 (May 1959): 350; Yamaguchi Kazuo, *Meiji zenki keizai no bunseki* (Tokyo, 1956), p. 60.

5. Tōbata Seiichi, *Nōchi o meguru jinushi to nōmin* (Tokyo, 1947), p. 72; Ono *Nōson shi,* p. 333. According to Ono, most applicants to secondary schools specializing in agriculture were sons of former samurai and landlords or individuals who had failed to gain entrance to regular middle or normal schools. Ordinary farmers lacked both the means and the interest to educate their sons in agricultural science.

6. He also was active in promoting afforestation and land reclamation. Denda Isao, "Kokuminshugi shisō to nōhonshugi shisō," in *Meiji zenhan ki no nashonarizumu,* ed. Sakata Yoshio (Tokyo, 1958), pp. 267-68.

7. Kondō Yasuo, *Mura no kōzō* (Tokyo, 1955), p. 267.

various crops, and, as Ekita had done, on finding ways of controlling insects.[8]

Useful discoveries could be transmitted to their tenants by a variety of means. It was an accepted part of the landlords' role that they supervise their tenants' farming—as an old saying put it: "The trail made by landlords [through their tenants' fields] is the best fertilizer yet devised."[9] Given the authority landlords possessed, simply commanding their tenants to change farming techniques was often sufficient. Where innovations required greater labor or involved some degree of risk, however, economic incentives were important. A landlord in Gifu Prefecture promised to cover all losses if the advice he gave his tenants on ways to increase yields proved unsuccessful.[10] Others gave prizes of money or tools to tenants who produced superior crops.[11] But less tangible incentives could be equally effective. Tenants of a landlord in Yamagata Prefecture vied with each other in raising yields for the honor of attending a special New Year's party at the landlord's home and of receiving from him a ceremonial robe inscribed with the phrase "prosperity and welfare."[12] Elsewhere, the tenant who raised the best crops during the year was seated closest to the landlord at his year-end feast and addressed by him as "mister," a polite suffix landlords rarely used when speaking to tenants.[13]

8. Tōbata, *Nōchi o meguru*, p. 68; by the same author, "Nihon nōgyō hatten no ninaite," in Nōgyō hattatsu shi chōsa kai, ed., *Nihon nōgyō hattatsu shi* 9: 567–68; Ronald Dore, *Land Reform in Japan* (London, 1959), p. 46.

9. Quoted in Niigata ken nōkai, *Jinushi kosaku mondai ni taisuru jinushi no iken* (Niigata, 1921). A variant—"The landlord's footprints turn to dung"—is quoted in Dore, "Agricultural Improvement," p. 78.

10. J. W. Robertson Scott, *The Foundations of Japan* (London, 1922), p. 30.

11. Ibid., pp. 186–87.

12. Ibid., p. 187.

13. Dore, "Agricultural Improvement," p. 81. Of course, landlords could also employ their authority to obstruct agricultural improvement. The tenants of a landlord in Yamagata Prefecture, for example, presumably during the Taishō period, wanted to use machines for plowing. But the landlord had no interest in machines and let it be known that he considered it an egregious breach of etiquette "for one of the tenant's station to buy a luxury even the master doesn't own." As a result only the largest owner-cultivators in the village bought machines; tenants

Nor was the landlords' ability to stimulate improvements limited to their own tenants. They could influence owner-cultivators in their villages as well. As had been the case in the region of the rice stubble riot, most farmers in the early Meiji era resented official interference in their affairs; government efforts to promote agriculture were, they believed, merely veiled attempts to raise taxes. The motives of landlords, however, who were members of their own communities and whose families had often served as spokesmen for local interests for generations, were less suspect.[14] Sometimes the traditional prestige of landlords alone was enough to win acceptance of new techniques. More commonly, the demonstrated effectiveness of their innovations, revealed by higher yields and improved quality of crops on their own or their tenants' land, would convince others to try the same methods. Small owner-cultivators in particular, who could afford few risks themselves, looked to landlords for leadership in agricultural matters; until a new tool or a new procedure had been tested and proved beneficial by landlords, they were reluctant to adopt it themselves.[15]

Generally, larger landlords were in a better position than smaller landlords to promote agricultural improvements. In the first place, they had greater wealth at their disposal and were able individually

---

and many small cultivators who were dependent on the landlord in various ways yielded to the "master's will." Kondō, *Mura no kōzō,* pp. 58-60. In the early Meiji era, however, few landlords appear to have opposed improvements so vehemently.

14. By the turn of the century, the farmers' distrust of the government was largely overcome. The abandonment of plans to revise legal land values every five years made official encouragement of agricultural improvement less suspicious. The victory of Japan in the Sino-Japanese War of 1894-95, moreover, aroused considerable popular support for the regime, and by the early 1900s nationalism was becoming a potent force in rural society. During the Russo-Japanese War, one landlord used the national emergency as an incentive for agricultural improvement, advising his tenants that "on warm, cloudy days insects multiply rapidly. Think of your brothers at the front, struggling against one of the mighty military powers of the world, and be ashamed to be vanquished by hordes of insects or masses of weeds." Robertson Scott, *Foundations,* pp. 187-88. After the turn of the century, too, ordinary farmers became far more receptive to information about scientific farming techniques. See Dore, "Agricultural Improvement," p. 85.

15. See Sunaga Shigemitsu, ed., *Kindai Nihon no jinushi to nōmin* (Tokyo, 1966), pp. 249-50.

to provide the capital for land reclamation projects and for new irrigation and drainage facilities. To the extent that their holdings were concentrated in one area, they could enjoy economies of scale as well in any project they undertook. In addition, the more concentrated their holdings, the more likely it was that they provided all the land their tenants cultivated, making it easier for them to supervise the introduction of new methods.[16] In contrast, smaller landlords, especially those whose holdings were scattered about in tiny parcels, found it necessary to work out plans for land improvement projects with others, and the opposition of even one neighboring landowner could stymie negotiations for months. Their tenants usually rented land from other landlords as well, sometimes from as many as a dozen.[17] While tenants may have thereby gained some measure of protection from arbitrary treatment, agricultural improvement clearly suffered. Tenants might be urged by one of their landlords to use a new fertilizer and forbidden to do so by another, or told to plant a new strain of rice in which no one else had confidence. In such confused circumstances, productivity was more apt to decrease than increase.[18] To the extent that smaller landlords could cooperate with one another in planning improvements and in coordinating policy toward their tenants, these disadvantages could be overcome; but on the whole it appears that their contributions were less, in both extent and importance, than those of larger landlords.

The motives of landlords in promoting improvements were diverse. For some landlords, taking an interest in local farming was

16. John D. Eyre, "The Changing Role of the Former Japanese Landlord," *Land Economics* 31 (February 1955): 39.

17. Tōbata, *Nōchi o meguru*, pp. 64–65; for information on the number of landlords from whom tenants rented land, see Arimoto Hideo, "Kosakunō no zokusuru jinushi sū ni tsuite," *Teikoku nōkai hō* 11 (October 1921): 9–13.

18. Recognizing that the complexity of tenancy relations hindered agricultural improvement and upset landlord-tenant harmony, officials in Ehime Prefecture recommended in 1918 that "landlords should aim at having as few tenants as possible, and tenants should try to lease land from only one landlord." Ehime ken naimubu, *Beikoku kensa jisshi no kosaku ni oyoboshitaru eikyō* (Matsuyama, 1932), p. 61.

simply a matter of course, a role dictated by tradition which both they and their tenants took for granted. Others were motivated by reformist zeal. Shibusawa Sōsuke, a landlord in Saitama Prefecture, discovered new techniques for raising silkworms and producing greater numbers of cocoons. But rather than keeping his findings secret, thereby profiting only himself, he chose to tell others about them. He was, one gathers from the introduction to the explanatory manual he had printed, "motivated by the desire to overcome the fatalistic attitude of the common peasant who only followed techniques hallowed by custom and entrusted the final outcome to benign Providence."[19]

Patriotism seems to have been the major motive behind Okada's experiments with sorghum. Believing that the loss of specie was "a great disease of the nation," he sought to lessen the country's dependence on imported sugar.[20] In addition, like Shibusawa, he wanted to overcome the fatalistic attitude of farmers and helped organize a local agricultural society in 1878 aimed at making "all the people of the district . . . students of agricultural science."[21] Similar organizations were being formed by landlords throughout the country.[22]

But self-interest was probably the most powerful motive, and one which affected all landlords, both large and small. As illustrations, consider the role of landlords in establishing rice inspection (*bei-koku kensa*) and in carrying out land adjustment (*kōchi seiri*).

Rice Inspection

As noted previously, the Meiji land settlement eliminated all controls on farming and farmers which had been imposed by the Tokugawa regime. But the new government by no means lost interest in agriculture. Not only was the land tax its major source of income; agricultural products such as tea, silk and silkworm eggs

19. William J. Chambliss, *Chiaraijima Village: Land Tenure, Taxation and Local Trade 1818–1884* (Tucson, 1965), p. 19.
20. Denda, "Kokuminshugi shisō," pp. 267, 269.
21. Ibid., p. 268.
22. Tōbata, *Nōchi o meguru*, p. 71.

were also the country's major export items in the Meiji era and a vital source of foreign currency to pay for imported machinery and raw materials.[23] Like Tokugawa officials before them, the Meiji leaders continued to regard agriculture as the basis of the nation's prosperity, and they remained concerned with encouraging higher agricultural productivity. They believed, however, that agricultural improvements could be brought about by laissez faire rather than by coercion and direct governmental supervision of farming. As Matsukata Masayoshi, chief architect of the new land tax, observed in 1878: ". . . by granting rights of ownership to the people, their love of the land is increased, and they become diligent students of farming."[24]

His statement, however, reflected the government's hopes, not the realities of the situation, for the immediate effects of the land settlement were just the opposite of what had been intended. Although yields may have increased slightly in the 1870s and 1880s, the quality of crops deteriorated. The quality of rice in particular, the nation's most important crop, declined markedly.[25] There were several reasons for this.

One of the most important measures employed by the government during the Tokugawa period to control agriculture was the inspection of tax rice. Typically, official inspectors withdrew a few handfuls of rice from every bale to look for impurities or signs of dampness. If the rice did not meet established standards, it was either rejected or penalty payments were levied on the offending taxpayers. The bales themselves were also examined for their strength and durability. These strict measures were necessary to prevent excessive loss of rice during shipment from the villages to government warehouses and to make sure that rice paid to samurai or stored for famine relief did not decompose before it was needed. They also

---

23. Ono, *Nōson shi,* pp. 217-18.
24. Matsukata Masayoshi, "Chisō shi," in Ōkurashō, ed., *Meiji zenki zaisei keizai shiryō shūsei* 1 (Tokyo, 1933): 371. For a general discussion of the evolution of the government's agricultural policy in the years 1868 through 1889, see Ono, *Nōson shi,* pp. 221-34.
25. Ibid., pp. 525-26.

served to guarantee the reputation of tax rice in the markets of Osaka and Edo where many daimyo, hard-pressed for cash in the latter part of the Tokugawa period, sold surplus stocks.[26]

The majority of farmers, however, sold little rice themselves; most of what they retained after taxes was used for their own consumption. Fearful of invoking the displeasure of officials, they attempted to meet quality standards for tax rice, but they saw little reason to be concerned with the quality of the rest of their crop. Careful baling was unnecessary since no transport was involved; impurities could be removed as the rice was used. When official inspection was eliminated at the time of the land settlement, farmers no longer thought it necessary to maintain quality standards, not realizing that the marketplace could be as harsh a judge of quality as tax officials had been in the past.[27]

The repeal of sumptuary laws regulating the dress, diet, and deportment of farmers and the removal of all restrictions on choice of occupation may also have contributed to the deterioration of rice quality. As a government report observed in 1884, many farmers were too busy enjoying their new freedom to pay much attention to farming:

In keeping with current fashions, people who used to be farmers have become peddlers and local merchants. If, because of their inexperience, they fail at business, they go back to farming for a while. Since they can go anywhere and do whatever they wish, they lack purpose and end up doing nothing well. Until recently, moreover, restaurants, bars, and clothing stores could only be found in castle towns, but now one finds foreign goods even in the most remote regions. Young farmers have abandoned straw raincoats for fancy cloaks. . . . Without knowing it, they become addicted to luxury.[28]

Probably of more importance than the farmers' sense of release from old obligations, however, was the new obligation imposed by the land settlement: the payment of taxes in cash. According to one

---

26. Ogura Takekazu, "Meiji zenki nōsei no dōkō to nōkai no seiritsu," in *Nihon nōgyō hattatsu shi* 3: 319; Ono, *Nōson shi,* p. 525.

27. Ibid., p. 526.

28. Quoted in Ogura, "Nōsei no dōkō," pp. 321–22.

estimate, merely to obtain money for taxes the average farmer in the 1870s had to market at least 30 percent of his crop. Adding to that the money he needed to buy tools and fertilizer, he had to market 50 percent.[29] In many parts of the country, however, neither the demand nor the facilities for such substantial transactions existed. Local prices were low and, lacking access to major urban markets, the farmer's only hope was to sell as much rice as possible at whatever price he could obtain. Careful threshing and drying, while insuring the quality of rice, inevitably caused some reduction in its volume, a luxury he could not afford. He became less concerned with quality, therefore, than with quantity.

The inflation of the late 1870s did not solve the problem. Rice prices rose sharply, outstripping price increases for fertilizer and other necessities. As a result, the farmers' tax burden—the amount of rice they were compelled to sell each year—decreased. Even so, rice quality continued to deteriorate. Farmers who had been forced to borrow money to pay taxes a few years before now had an opportunity to liquidate their debts. Others took advantage of higher prices to amass capital for buying more land. Although it is extreme to say that farmers became "addicted to luxury," no doubt many of them saw rising rice prices as a means of improving their standard of living. In short, although no longer compelled to sell large quantities of rice, they now chose to do so.[30] Many began planting autumn rice, a variety which took longer to mature, required less attention, and produced higher yields than ordinary rice. Autumn rice had been prohibited throughout most of the country before the Restoration, and with good reason: not only was it particularly vulnerable to damage from typhoons in the late summer, but also in the cool weather following the belated harvest it could not be

---

29. Ogura Takekazu, *Tochi rippō no shiteki kōsatsu* (Tokyo, 1951), pp. 126–27.
30. See, for example, the report on conditions in Hyogo Prefecture in Ogura, "Nōsei no dōkō," p. 323. The problem of quality was also severe in northern Kyushu where the demand for rice, stimulated by the presence of thousands of imperial troops after the abortive uprising of Saigo Takamori in 1877, far surpassed local supply, impelling dealers there to buy any kind of rice they could obtain. Kamagata Isao, *Yamagata ken inasaku shi* (Tokyo, 1953), pp. 96–97.

thoroughly dried, making it unsafe for storage. But in their haste for profit, farmers overlooked these problems.[31]

By the early 1880s the harmful effects of the deterioration of rice quality on the economy were apparent. Rice purchased from farmers spoiled before it could be sold. In Miyagi Prefecture in 1884, for example, 20,000 *koku* of poorly dried rice rotted in local storehouses before dealers could arrange its sale in Tokyo.[32] Elsewhere dealers mixed good rice with bad and sold it to their unsuspecting customers.[33] As a result of fraudulent practices, public confidence in the rice market declined. A large number of industrial rice consumers, notably sake brewers, were forced to curtail production or raise prices because of the shortage of good quality rice.[34]

The government, although alarmed by this state of affairs, was reluctant to reestablish official inspection of crops, a step which some rice brokers in Tokyo strongly recommended, fearing both the financial burden it would impose on the state and the resentment it would undoubtedly arouse among farmers so recently emancipated from government controls. Believing, however, that some form of regulation was necessary, the government urged all people connected with the rice trade—producers, dealers, and retailers—to start their own inspection programs. Unwilling to compel inspection by law, it nevertheless issued a set of guidelines for voluntary trade associations in 1884 and instructed prefectural officials to encourage their formation.[35]

Most urban rice brokers responded favorably to this plan, realizing that quick profits were no substitute for a stable market. They launched a campaign to eliminate fraudulent selling practices and established quality standards for the rice they purchased from farmers, offering substantially higher prices for good rice as an incentive to improvement. Rice purchases from regions with a poor reputation for quality declined.[36]

31. Ogura, "Nōsei no dōkō," p. 320.
32. Ibid.
33. Ibid.
34. Ibid.; Ono, *Nōson shi*, p. 526.
35. Ogura, "Nōsei no dōkō," pp. 327–29.
36. Ono, *Nōson shi*, pp. 526–27.

Landlords were also among the first to adopt the idea of voluntary inspection. There is some evidence of concern on their part for regional prosperity and the welfare of local farmers, but their primary motive was self-interest since the quality of rent rice had also deteriorated after the Restoration.

During the Tokugawa period there were three different systems for paying taxes on tenanted land. Under the most common system, the tenant took all but his own share of the rice crop to his landlord who then paid what was due in taxes, keeping the remainder for himself. Under the second, the rice was divided by the tenant into the tax and rent payments and delivered by him to the village tax office and to his landlord. Under the third, the tenant took both tax rice and rent rice to the village office; after the rice had been inspected and taxes deducted, the landlord was able to claim his share.[37]

Although precise information is lacking, it appears that the third system prevailed in rice-exporting regions of the country. It was, first of all, advantageous for the daimyo who were assured of having first claim on the rice crop, and was often enforced by them in order to guarantee the speedy collection of tax rice. Secondly, it benefited landlords. Since all the rice delivered by tenants was inspected, they were certain that their rent rice met the standards imposed by the government. Even where not required by the daimyo this system was sometimes put into effect by village officials, who might well be landlords themselves.[38] But official controls on rent rice disappeared with the elimination of inspection in 1873. Tenants, like owner-cultivators, had regarded inspection as a political necessity; once freed from it, they, too, became negligent about the rice they produced.

Moreover, the majority of tenants throughout the country also owned some land of their own. According to a survey made in 1883,

37. Ono Takeo, *Meiji zenki tochi seido shiron* (Tokyo, 1948), pp. 157–62; Ogura, *Tochi rippō,* pp. 79–81.
38. Ibid., p. 80.

47

landless tenants accounted for only 22 percent of all farm house-holds; 39 percent of the total were owner-cultivators; the remaining 39 percent were owner-tenants.[39] Owner-tenants formed a diverse group: tenants who had acquired a small parcel of their own land; owner-cultivators who were in the process of selling their land piece by piece to pay debts but who had remained on it as tenants; and other owner-cultivators who leased additional land in order to utilize surplus family labor.[40] Although the landless tenant did not sell much of his produce, the owner-tenant was forced to by the new land tax. Like the pure owner-cultivator, he, too, was tempted to grow as much rice as he could, both on his own and on his rented holding, in order to increase his marketable surplus—and with the same effects on the quality of the crops he raised.

Initially few landlords were concerned about the inferior quality of rent rice. Some no doubt were just as guilty as owner-cultivators of seeking quick profits during the inflation. But as rice prices began to decline in the early 1880s, in response to the new policies of the major rice exchanges and, more importantly, to the Matsukata deflation, landlords became alarmed. By 1884 rice prices had fallen to 4.8 yen per *koku,* half their level in 1880; in effect, the burden of the land tax doubled. As the elite of rural society, landlords were usually the first people contacted by prefectural officials anxious to improve local rice quality and the first to become aware of the new quality standards imposed by brokers. Moreover, some landlords were themselves local rice dealers and knew firsthand the problems of storing and shipping inferior rice. They depended heavily on sales of rice in major cities where, as a rule, prices were highest, and were afraid of being shut out of these lucrative markets.

But there were limits to what any one landlord could do to improve either the quality of his rent rice or the prices he received. If his holding was scattered, it was likely that his tenants rented land

39. Nōchi kaikaku kiroku iinkai, ed., *Nōchi kaikaku tenmatsu gaiyō* (Tokyo, 1951), p. 34.

40. Dore, *Land Reform,* p. 18; Dorothy Orchard, "Agrarian Problems of Modern Japan," *Journal of Political Economy* 37 (April 1929): 138-39.

from other landlords as well. If he alone imposed standards for rent rice, or imposed more rigorous standards than other landlords, his tenants were apt to protest, claiming that he was demanding more labor from them, in effect raising rents. Moreover, prices were determined on a regional basis and were not apt to rise until the reputation of all local rice improved. Therefore, a landlord interested in increasing his own profits from the sale of rice had to seek the cooperation not only of other landlords, but also of all local rice producers, and this led him to support the kind of voluntary inspection programs the government recommended in 1884. The rice improvement campaign in the Shōnai region of Yamagata Prefecture is a case in point.

The Shōnai plain, located in the northwestern part of the prefecture, is one of the largest unbroken stretches of arable land in Japan. Thirty miles long from north to south and fifteen miles wide, it is bordered on three sides by mountains and on the fourth by the Japan Sea. Throughout the Meiji and Taishō periods farming remained the principal occupation of the population and rice the most important crop. In the 1880s almost 80 percent of the land, some 31,500 of 40,000 *chō,* was paddy, producing well over 400,000 *koku* of rice each year, an amount far exceeding the needs of local farmers.[41]

That so much land was devoted to rice cultivation was largely the result of agricultural policies enforced by the Sakai, daimyo of Shōnai domain from 1622 until the Restoration. Under their leadership, extensive reclamation and irrigation projects were completed; crops other than rice were discouraged.[42] Part of the surplus which was created was stored in emergency granaries. But most of it was used to increase domain income from the lucrative rice trade with southwestern Japan which had developed in the late seventeenth

41. Kamagata, *Inasaku shi,* pp. 378-79. The official yield of Shōnai domain at the end of the Tokugawa period was roughly 190,000 *koku* of rice, but actual yields were much higher—according to one estimate, over 400,000 *koku.* See Oikawa Shirō, ed., *Yamagata ken nōchi kaikaku shi* (Yamagata, 1953), pp. 22-23.
42. Kamagata, *Inasaku shi,* pp. 32-41.

century. Indeed, the existence of this trade was the most important reason behind efforts to increase rice production.

In 1671 the *bakufu* opened a sea route from Sakata, a coastal town in the northern part of the plain, to Edo by way of Kyushu and the Inland Sea. At first most of the rice shipped from Sakata came from *bakufu* territories in the area and was sent directly to the capital. But within twenty years the daimyo of nearby domains began shipping surplus rice along the same route, taking advantage of increased demand for rice in such rapidly growing cities as Kyoto and Osaka. No one was more active in this trade than the Sakai. In 1724 over half the rice shipped from Sakata came from Shōnai.[43]

In promoting the rice trade with southwestern Japan, the Sakai were interested not only in increasing the quantity of rice they could sell, but in maintaining its quality as well. All cultivators, including tenants, were required to take their tax rice to local government warehouses for inspection. Strict standards of dryness and baling were enforced to prevent loss or spoilage during the long sea voyage to the marketplace. If an inspector found as few as three grains of unhulled rice in the sample he took from each bale, he was under orders to reject the whole bale. As a final precaution, both the inspector and the taxpayer had to sign their names to a slip of paper attached to each bale which passed inspection.[44]

Only after this process was completed, in mid-December, were landlords allowed to collect rent rice. In this way the domain was certain of claiming its share of the crop first. In addition, by

---

43. Ibid., pp. 43–44. Kamagata notes that in addition to enriching the Sakai, the rice trade also provided commoners in the domain with an opportunity to acquire wealth. Some of the tax rice was carried in ships owned by the government, but merchant ships were also used. For each one hundred bales of rice carried, the merchants received from twenty-two to twenty-five bales, or alternatively, about 20 *ryō* in cash. When harvests were good, they could buy rice directly from local farmers and carry it along with their consignments of tax rice to the ports they visited. Many of these merchants used their profits to acquire land. The Homma family, for example, began as rice merchants in Sakata in the late 1600s. By the end of the Tokugawa period they controlled over 1,500 *chō* of land in the Shōnai plain.

44. Ogura, "Nōsei no dōkō," pp. 319–20.

officially recognizing the cultivator, whether owner or tenant, as the taxpayer, it retained direct control over farming and could prevent landlords from interfering with its agricultural policies. As long as the government demanded taxes in rice, for example, landlords could not persuade their tenants to plant other crops.

But in Nishitagawa and Higashitagawa *gun,* the major rice producing regions of the domain,[45] officials adopted an even stricter policy. Tenants there were required to take both tax rice and rent rice to the warehouses. After the rice was inspected tax officials settled accounts with the landlords. Exactly how this settlement was made is not known, but in at least some cases landlords received a cash payment instead of rice, the amount being determined by current local rice prices.[46]

This policy had obvious advantages for the landlords concerned. If they were paid in rice, they were sure of its quality. Moreover, they could collect their rents at the warehouses rather than from individual tenants scattered throughout the countryside, saving themselves (or more likely, their tenants) considerable time and labor. If paid in cash, no transportation was necessary at all and a fair profit from the sale of their rice was assured. It is unlikely, however, that officials adopted this policy solely to suit the convenience of landlords. It had advantages for the government as well, chiefly in providing it with a reserve supply of inspected, and therefore marketable, rice. If demand for rice in Osaka increased, the government could buy the landlords' share and add it to its own shipment of tax rice.

The Meiji land settlement proved a mixed blessing for the landlords in these two districts. On the one hand, like all landlords, they gained clear title to their land and, since they now received both the rental and tax portions of their tenants' crops, were in a position to sell larger quantities of rice than before. On the other hand, they lost the system of controls which had guaranteed the

45. Kamagata, *Inasaku shi,* p. 99.
46. Ibid., p. 386.

quality and commercial value of that rice. During the 1870s the quality of their rent rice, like all rice produced in the region, grew progressively worse.[47]

To improve quality individual landlords at first imposed their own inspection. One such landlord was Hirata Yasukichi, who later became a leader of the rice improvement campaign in the Shōnai plain.

Originally the Hirata were peddlers of dry goods in Ise. When they arrived in the Shōnai plain is not known, but by 1622, when Sakai Tadayoshi took over as daimyo of Shōnai *han,* they were wealthy enough to provide housing for his retainers in Tsuruoka, the castle town.[48] At the time of the Restoration they owned about 50 *chō* of paddy. How and when it was acquired is also not known, but from fragmentary records it appears that a sizable portion of their holding dated from the late seventeenth century.[49]

Yasukichi, born in 1857, assumed the headship of his family in 1879. By 1883 he acquired an additional 40 or 50 *chō* of land, most of it paddy, making his total holding roughly 100 *chō*. His land was scattered throughout the countryside around Tsuruoka. About half, the portion his family had acquired before the Restoration, was spread among eight villages in Nishitagawa *gun*; the other, newly acquired half was spread among nine villages in Higashitagawa *gun*.[50]

Each year he received roughly 1,000 *koku* of rice as rents. No longer able to benefit from official inspection, he hired a team of millers every year to polish the rice, instructing them to examine its quality as they worked. Like the tax officials before him, he was especially strict about dampness, and if any poorly dried rice was discovered he demanded that the tenant replace it.[51]

47. Ibid., pp. 97–99, 101–2.
48. Koyama Magojirō, "Meiji ni okeru jinushi no nōji kairyō undō," in *Nihon nōgyō hattatsu shi* 5: 602.
49. Ibid., pp. 604–5.
50. Ibid., pp. 601, 605–6.
51. Ibid., p. 612.

But his efforts, and similar efforts by other landlords, had little effect on prices. Since roughly 60 percent of the paddy in the region was farmed by owner-cultivators,[52] the rice they sold had a greater impact on the market and on the reputation of Shōnai rice than the rice sold by landlords. At first the landlords tried to circumvent this difficulty by cooperating to promote the reputation and sale of rent rice, to convince dealers, especially those in Tokyo where prices were highest, that their rent rice was in fact superior to Shōnai rice generally. This they did by means of the Regulations for the Improvement and Trading of Shōnai Rice, issued in 1884. All owners of land worth 10,000 yen or more—in terms of legal land values for the region, holdings of at least 25 *chō*[53]—agreed to make at least one-tenth of their rent rice meet the quality standards outlined in the regulations by 1885. That rice would be delivered to selected local dealers and, if it passed their inspection, would receive a tag identifying it as improved Shōnai rice. The quality standards imposed by the regulations reflected the landlords' awareness of the criticisms dealers were making about Shōnai rice. All rice was to be dried thoroughly and threshed twice to remove impurities. Bales were to be made of two layers instead of one to eliminate leakage and, in response to complaints that they were too heavy for easy handling, were to be reduced in capacity from 5 to 4.2 *to.*[54]

A good plan in theory, it did not work well in practice. It was still necessary for landlords to inspect their tenants' rent payments themselves. In addition, they had to pay a fee for subsequent inspection by local dealers. And although improved Shōnai rice did receive a higher price in Tokyo, the local dealers who handled its sale gained most of the increment as commissions. Since the whole system depended on the certification of rice quality by dealers, direct sales of inspected rice by landlords on the Tokyo exchange were impossible.

52. Kamagata, *Inasaku shi,* p. 380.
53. Koyama, "Nōji kairyō undō," pp. 615–16.
54. Ibid., pp. 613–15. One *to* equals one-tenth of a *koku,* or roughly half a bushel of rice.

At this point, Yasukichi suggested an alternative approach to the problem of rice quality: the formation of rice improvement associations in each district of the region to which all farmers, not just landlords, would belong. The associations themselves would conduct inspection, replacing dealers as the guarantors of local rice quality. His suggestion was adopted, and by 1889 the associations were in operation throughout most of the plain.[55]

The results were as anticipated. Once all farmers were included in the campaign, the general level of rice quality improved, leading to increased demand and higher prices for Shōnai rice on the major exchanges. With the establishment of local inspection facilities landlords were freed of the expense and inconvenience of inspecting rent rice themselves. By 1890, for example, Yasukichi abandoned his own inspection program, directing his tenants to deliver rents to the nearest branch of the improvement association instead.[56] Moreover, although many landlords still sold their rent rice through local dealers, they could if they chose sell directly to Tokyo. By pooling their stocks of inspected rice and bypassing local middlemen, a group of large landlords in Higashitagawa *gun* increased their profits on the rice they sold in 1889 by over 6 percent.[57]

The success of rice improvement associations in the Shōnai plain of Yamagata and in a few other prefectures during the 1890s[58] in improving both the quality and price of local rice encouraged the formation of improvement associations elsewhere, especially in the major rice-exporting regions of the country. By the end of the Meiji period inspection programs were functioning in thirty prefectures.[59] To eliminate the potentially harmful effects of local political and personal rivalries and to promote greater efficiency of operation, most of these programs were now run by prefectural officials and

---

55. Ibid., pp. 616–17; Kamagata, *Inasaku shi,* pp. 102–3.

56. Koyama, "Nōji kairyō undō," p. 612; also, the report from the Sakata Rice Exchange in Kamagata, *Inasaku shi,* p. 252.

57. Ibid., pp. 103–4.

58. For a discussion of early efforts to establish rice inspection elsewhere than in Yamagata, see Ogura, "Nōsei no dōkō," pp. 329–34.

59. "Taishō gannen honpō kosaku chōsa shiryō," reprinted in Nōrinshō, nōmukyoku, *Honpō kosaku kankō* (Tokyo, 1926), p. 130.

required that all rice destined for commercial sale undergo inspection.[60]

As in the Shōnai plain, inspection brought landlords throughout the country considerable rewards. They demanded not only that tenants deliver rent rice to inspection facilities, but also that the rice meet at least the minimum standards of commercial quality.[61] Able to store rice safely, they could wait until late summer and early fall when prices were usually highest, to sell it.[62] Since most landlords sold a substantial portion of the rent rice they received and, as a group, provided roughly half the total volume of rice on the commercial market after the turn of the century,[63] they were in a position to profit handsomely from the price increases which inspection helped bring about.

In contrast, inspection offered few if any direct economic benefits to tenants. Because they sold relatively little rice themselves,[64] they were unable to profit from higher prices. Furthermore, meeting the standards of quality for rent rice imposed by their landlords required extra work on their part in drying and threshing rice and in manufacturing suitable bales.[65] Most landlords realized this and

---

60. For a discussion of the shift in the early 1900s from private to public inspection, see Ono, *Nōson shi*, pp. 526-30. See also "Taishō junen honpō kosaku kankō," in *Honpō kosaku kankō*, pp. 287-89, for information on the various types of inspection in effect in the early 1920s.

61. "Taishō gannen kosaku kankō," pp. 130, 131-35.

62. Yagi Yoshinosuke, *Beikoku tōsei ron* (Tokyo, 1934), pp. 8-9. Landlords were not, it should be stressed, guaranteed of maximizing their profits if they waited until the so-called "lean period" to sell their rice. See Matsumoto Hiroshi, "Meiji Taishō ki ni okeru jinushi no beikoku hanbai ni tsuite," *Hitotsubashi ronsō* 60:5 (1968): 547-65, for a well-documented study of the risks involved in selling rice.

63. Yagi, *Beikoku tōsei ron*, pp. 6-8; *Nōchi kaikaku tenmatsu gaiyō*, p. 35.

64. How much rice a tenant farmer sold each year depended, among other things, on how much cash he needed to pay for fertilizer and other essential items and on whether or not he had other sources of cash income at his disposal. Most writers agree that after the turn of the century tenants as a whole 1) sold little of the rice they produced, perhaps 15% at most, 2) sold the greater part of it by January, that is, during the period when prices usually were lowest, and 3) sometimes sold part of the rice they needed for their own consumption because they required immediate cash. See Ogura, *Tochi rippō*, p. 140; Dore, *Land Reform*, pp. 38-39; Yagi, *Beikoku tōsei ron*, pp. 8-9.

65. Ehime ken naimubu, *Beikoku kensa jisshi*, pp. 69-86; "Taishō jūnen kosaku kankō," pp. 289-92.

either from a sense of fairness or from fear of disputes provided "bonuses" of rice or cash for each bale of inspected rice they received as rent. Usually amounting to only a few *shō* per *koku* of rice, however, these "bonuses" merely compensated tenants for their added labor.[66] They broke even while their landlords reaped increased profits from the sale of rice.

Because tenants gained nothing, many writers have condemned rice inspection as an example of the landlords' "parasitism."[67] This view, however, disregards the socially useful consequences of inspection—its salutary effects on the rice market and the impetus it gave to the commercialization of other crops. Although superficially similar to inspection during the Tokugawa period, inspection programs established during the Meiji period depended not on political pressure for their success but on the profit motive. Substantially higher prices for superior grades of rice gave farmers a positive incentive to improve their crops—to develop better strains of rice and new techniques for processing rice after the harvest. Once aware of the economic advantages of improving rice quality, they were stimulated to promote the commercial quality of their secondary crops as well.[68] With the creation of uniform national standards for quality and baling, the rice market widened. Rice from remote regions could be shipped to distant cities with little fear of leakage or spoilage, making farmers less dependent on local demand and insuring an adequate food supply for the rapidly expanding urban population. Once forced to mortgage their land when they needed immediate cash, farmers could now use rice as collateral for loans.[69]

66. "Taishō gannen kosaku kankō," pp. 131-35; "Taishō jūnen kosaku kankō," pp. 292-95. One *shō* equals one-tenth of a *to,* or one-hundredth of a *koku.*
67. For criticisms of rice inspection, see Nōmin undō shi kenkyū kai, *Nihon nōmin undō shi* (Tokyo, 1961), p. 405; Wakukawa Seiyei, "The Japanese Farm Tenancy System," in *Japan's Prospect,* ed. D. G. Haring (Cambridge, Mass., 1946), pp. 145-46; Helen Miller, "Government Rice Inspection and Tenant Disputes in the Taishō Period" (unpublished paper presented at the Midwest Japan Seminar, December 1972).
68. Ono, *Nōson shi,* p. 531.
69. Ibid., p. 532; "Taishō jūnen kosaku kankō," p. 296.

Land Adjustment

Another example of landlord efforts to improve agriculture, again motivated by self-interest, was land adjustment. Aimed both at expanding the area of arable land and improving land already under cultivation, land adjustment involved the consolidation of fragmented, irregularly shaped plots into larger, rectangular units; the concurrent straightening of roads, levees, and field paths; and the construction of new ditches, reservoirs, and other facilities for efficient irrigation and drainage.

Beginning in 1899 the government took an active interest in land adjustment, offering a variety of tax incentives to landowners who carried out adjustment projects, compelling dissenting landowners to participate in projects which the majority agreed upon, and providing both technical and financial aid. Its efforts, stemming from concern over the ability of the agricultural sector to supply increased domestic demand for food, were well rewarded. By 1940 over one million *chō* of land, most of it paddy, had been adjusted. As anticipated, adjusted land proved more productive than unimproved land. Because of efficient drainage, paddy fields in all but the northernmost regions of the country could be converted to dry fields after the rice harvest, making double-cropping possible on what had once been single-crop land. Improved irrigation systems allowed farmers to control the flooding of paddy fields more accurately to achieve optimum growing conditions for young rice plants. Larger, regularly-shaped plots facilitated the use of horses—and later, machines—for plowing, permitting more effective working of the soil. According to one estimate, the total gain in yield per *tan* of rice in paddy fields from 1900 to 1935 was 0.39 *koku,* of which 0.24 *koku* (62 percent of the total gain) can be credited to adjustment. Thus, since over one million *chō* were adjusted, by 1940 the annual yield of rice was more than 2.4 million *koku* greater than it had been in 1900 as a consequence of adjustment alone.[70]

70. James Nakamura, *Agricultural Production and the Economic Development of Japan, 1873–1922* (Princeton, 1966), pp. 197–214.

Over 40 percent of the land adjusted after 1899 was tenanted.[71] But even before the government began to encourage adjustment, landlords were active in promoting it. Indeed, their experiments in land improvement and the effectiveness of the projects they carried out before 1899 helped convince the government of the value of a concerted national program for land adjustment.[72]

Some of these early attempts at adjustment were motivated by the landlords' desire to promote Western farming techniques, especially the use of draft animals on large-scale holdings.[73] But most were intended to increase the income of landlords without substantial alteration of the prevailing system of small-scale, labor-intensive farming. Adjustment was favored by landlords for three reasons.

First, it helped prevent decreases in the volume of rents they were able to collect. As noted earlier, although rents are commonly cited as a percentage of the harvest in secondary sources, in actual practice tenancy agreements (both written and oral) usually called for the payment of a specified quantity of rice as rent. The amount agreed upon, moreover, represented a maximum figure. By custom, the landlord could not raise rents if the harvest in a given year was better than normal; the increment in yield went to the tenant instead. But if the harvest was poor, as the result of a natural disaster and not negligence, the landlord was expected to reduce rents accordingly. In the late nineteenth century in particular, when crop failures were common, it was not unusual for landlords to be forced to grant reductions year after year and occasionally to find themselves unable to collect rents at all.[74] The need to provide their tenants with emergency food supplies or seed for the next year's crop was an additional cost at times.

71. Ibid., p. 208, note 36.
72. Ogawa Makoto, "Chisui suiri tochi kairyō no taikeiteki seibi," *Nihon nōgyō hattatsu shi* 4: 212.
73. Koyama, "Nōji kairyō undō," pp. 607–8.
74. The Sasaki of Miyagi Prefecture, for example, were unable to collect any rents in 1875; in 1879 they collected only 26 percent. Sunaga, *Kindai Nihon no jinushi,* p. 174.

If the damage inflicted by natural disasters could be minimized, landlords would not have to grant reductions, and their rental income would be stable, enabling them to take full advantage of rising rice prices. One of the most effective measures at their disposal was land adjustment which, by improving irrigation and drainage, greatly reduced the threat of drought or flooding, two major causes of poor yields.

Second, adjustment enabled landlords to increase their rental income without actually raising rents. Before adjustment many fields were actually larger than their registered area, either because their irregular shape prevented accurate measurement or because landowners, hoping for lower taxes, deliberately underreported the size of their fields at the time of the tax reform.[75] When the fields were resurveyed after adjustment, however, these differences between actual and registered area were uncovered. The elimination of unnecessary footpaths, the more rational placement of irrigation ditches, and the incorporation of previously unusable land also increased the area of adjusted fields.[76]

Generally, the amount of rent tenants paid was based on the registered area of the land they cultivated. Thus, just as landlords enjoyed tax savings from underreported land, tenants enjoyed rent savings. But with adjustment these rent savings disappeared. Even if rent per *tan* remained the same, the amount of rent landlords received per plot of land increased.[77]

Third, adjustment gave landlords an opportunity to raise rents in the future. As noted previously, the maximum amount of rent landlords could collect in any year was set forth in tenancy agreements. But, except for permanent tenancy contracts, these agreements remained in effect for only three to five years.[78] When they were renewed, landlords could and did demand higher rents. Since the

---

75. Dore, *Land Reform*, p. 37; Nakamura, *Agricultural Production*, pp. 22-37.
76. "Taishō gannen kosaku kankō," p. 123.
77. Ibid.; "Taishō jūnen kosaku kankō," p. 284.
78. Ono, *Nōson shi*, pp. 81, 83-84.

productivity of the land had increased, and since landlords could argue that they had contributed directly to that increase by bearing all or at least part of the costs of adjustment, their tenants had few grounds for complaint.[79] Indeed, tenants often contributed to rent increases themselves by competing with each other for improved land and offering to pay more in rent than was previously charged.[80]

In the Shōnai plain rent increases during a period when many adjustment projects were carried out absorbed most of the increase in the productivity of land. Average yields per *tan* rose from 2.25 *koku* in 1911 to 2.5 *koku* in 1916. Of this increase of .25 *koku*, however, .2 *koku* went to landlords in the form of higher rents; only .05 *koku* was retained by tenants.[81] But this was not always the case. In one village in Miyagi Prefecture where almost all arable land was adjusted, yields increased by .3 to .4 *koku* per *tan* between 1907 and the 1920s, yet rents increased by only .1 *koku*.[82] Tenants gained more from adjustment than landlords. Indeed, data on rent levels for the country as a whole in the late Meiji and Taishō periods indicate that rent increases lagged well behind increases in the productivity of land (Table 3). Thus, between the five-year periods 1908–12 and 1916–20, yields on single-crop paddy increased by .228 *koku* per *tan*, but rents increased by only .074 *koku* per *tan*. The tenant's share of the crop rose by .154 *koku* per *tan*, 68 percent of the increase in productivity. For double-crop paddy, yields increased by .136 *koku* per *tan*, but rents by only .039 *koku* per *tan*. The tenant's share of the crop rose by .097 *koku* per *tan*, 71 percent of the increase in productivity. Yields continued to increase through the 1930s, but as Table 3 indicates, rents now showed an absolute decline. This decline was caused, at least in part, by tenancy disputes, as will be discussed later.

79. "Taishō jūnen kosaku kankō," p. 284. The Land Adjustment Law of 1899 recognized the right of landlords to raise the rents when the productivity of land increased. Ogura, *Tochi rippō*, pp. 292–93.

80. "Taishō gannen kosaku kankō," p. 123.

81. Sato Shigemi, "Meiji Taishō ki ni okeru nōgyō gijitsu no hattatsu to haikei: Shōnai chihō no kanden bakō to kōchi seiri o chūshin to shite," *Nōgyō hattatsu shi chōsakai shiryō*, No. 89 (March 1954), pp. 88–89.

82. Sunaga, *Kindai Nihon no jinushi*, pp. 201–2, 211, 267.

TABLE 3.

Changes in Average Rent Levels
(excluding Hokkaido and Okinawa)[83]

	Single-crop paddy			Double-crop paddy		
	1908–12	1916–20	1933–35	1908–12	1916–20	1933–35
Yield/*tan* (in *koku*)	1.680	1.908	2.008	2.033	2.169	2.241
Rent/*tan* (in *koku*)	.898	.972	.920	1.156	1.195	1.116
Tenant's share/*tan* (in *koku*)	.782	.936	1.088	.877	.974	1.125

Source: Nōrinshō, *Nōchi mondai ni kansuru tōkei shiryō* (Tokyo, 1946), p. 23, reproduced in Nōmin undō shi kenkyū kai, ed., *Nihon nōmin undō shi* (Tokyo, 1961), p. 240 (Table 12).

A greater share of the harvest was not the only advantage tenants gained from land adjustment. Adjustment was often carried out in the immediate aftermath of natural disaster, and the wages tenants received for work on these projects helped sustain them until the next harvest.[84] Just as the greater security of farming once adjustment was completed reduced the need for landlords to grant rent reductions, it reduced the tenants' fear of famine. More important, improved irrigation facilities and the reshaping of fields into rectangular units simplified cultivation, reducing both the costs and labor requirements of farming. Less time was required to flood and drain paddy fields; rice could be planted and fertilized more efficiently; and sturdier levees and footpaths required less maintenance or repair. As a result, tenants could cultivate more land than before, provided land was available, or members of their families could seek part-time employment elsewhere.[85]

83. Based on surveys of average rent levels for medium-grade paddy.
84. Robertson Scott, *Foundations*, p. 197; Sunaga, *Kindai Nihon no jinushi*, pp. 202–3.
85. "Taishō gannen kosaku kankō," p. 126; "Taishō jūnen kosaku kankō," pp. 283–84.

The Effects of Agricultural Improvements on
Landlord-Tenant Relations

While bringing landlords immediate economic rewards, rice inspection, land adjustment, and most other agricultural improvements carried out during the Meiji era also affected landlord-tenant relations in ways that ultimately worked to the landlords' disadvantage.

During the first few decades of the Meiji era, and in many parts of the country during the Tokugawa period as well, tenants delivered rents directly to their landlords. To reward them for their labor and to encourage prompt payment, many landlords prepared a banquet for their tenants on the day rents were due.[86] Often the landlord himself appeared to make a speech praising the tenants for their hard work and to inquire after their health and family affairs. What might otherwise have been a sad day for tenants, who were, after all, parting with a large portion of their crop, thus became a festive occasion. For the moment, as they enjoyed plentiful food and drink, they forgot the burden which rents imposed on them. But as noted previously, after the establishment of inspection programs, most landlords directed their tenants to deliver rents to local warehouses instead.[87] Rather than an opportunity for feasting and social contact with landlords, the payment of rents was reduced to an impersonal economic obligation. At the warehouses tenants whose social world in the past had been confined to their own villages and whose major source of information about external affairs had been their own landlords now were able to meet tenants from the surrounding countryside, to exchange information on farming conditions, and, because of uniform regional standards for rice quality and baling, to compare rent levels. Some of them discovered that the rents they had taken for granted for so long were actually higher than those imposed by landlords elsewhere.

Like rice inspection, land adjustment also made the relationship

86. Ogura, *Tochi rippō*, pp. 313–14.
87. Ibid.; "Taishō jūnen kosaku kankō," p. 297.

between landlords and tenants more impersonal. In the past each landlord in a village had established his own rents on the basis of the quality, size and location of the parcels of land he owned; he might consider as well his tenants' past performance, or the length of time they had cultivated his land. But after adjustment, differences among parcels of land tended to diminish. Although soil conditions still varied somewhat, all paddy fields in a given area were now of roughly the same size, and all had virtually equal access to water. As a result, there was a tendency toward uniformity in rents. Indeed, in many communities landlords met together after adjustment was completed to agree upon rents for all land in the village; in some communities tenants also participated in the negotiations.[88] But whatever the procedure, the determination of rents became a collective, not an individual, matter.

Land adjustment did not eliminate crop failures entirely, but it brought an increased measure of security to farming. The wealth of landlords, once regarded by tenants as a guarantee of their own survival when disaster struck, now lost much of its functional significance. No longer as dependent on their landlords for emergency aid, tenants had less reason to be content with the great gap in living standards between landlords and themselves. In the past some tenants had been willing to pay extremely high rents to landlords with a reputation for granting generous rent reductions, sacrificing prosperity in good years for the comfort of knowing that when crops failed they would fare better than the tenants of less benevolent landlords. Now, however, they were more aware of the burden than the benefit of such high rents.

To the extent that adjustment and other improvements which increased the productivity of land brought not only security but also a greater share of the harvest to tenants, their dependence on landlords declined even further. At the same time, their attitude toward farming and the tenancy system itself—especially toward high rents in kind—underwent important changes.

88. "Taishō gannen kosaku kankō," pp. 124-25; "Taishō jūnen kosaku kankō," p. 283.

Many tenants were opposed to adjustment at first, partly for economic reasons—their fear, for example, that the reconstruction of levees and ditches, if not completed in time, would delay or perhaps prevent planting the next crop—but also for less rational reasons: for example, their sentimental attachment to a particular plot of land, perhaps one they had once owned or had tenanted for generations, which would in the course of adjustment change radically in appearance.[89] But they were, on the whole, favorably impressed by the results of adjustment, especially by the greater convenience of farming and the increased productivity of their land. Having seen that man could indeed improve upon nature in such an impressive manner, they became more enthusiastic about agricultural improvement in general and needed less prompting from their landlords to experiment with or adopt new techniques.[90] But the kind of improvements which tenants now became interested in were not always those which landlords willingly supported—for example, the creation of new field paths which would make farming even more convenient but which would have no effect on productivity or rents. Moreover, while landlords continued to emphasize improvements in the cultivation and processing of rice, the crop on which their wealth was based, tenants became more interested in raising yields of secondary crops.

As Table 3 indicates, rents were higher on double-crop than single-crop paddy. But in both cases rents were almost always payable in rice—that is, they were levied on the principal crop alone.[91] Thus, where adjustment made double-cropping possible or more rewarding than before, tenants naturally focused their attention on the secondary crop, hoping that by selling most of it they could offset the higher rents they usually had to pay on their rice crop and perhaps make a reasonable profit from farming.[92] But because demand for most secondary crops was highly elastic, prices

89. Robertson Scott, *Foundations*, p. 72.
90. "Taishō jūnen kosaku kankō," p. 285.
91. Ono, *Nōson shi*, p. 82; "Taishō gannen kosaku kankō," pp. 14–15, 18–20.
92. Ibid., p. 125 (example from Saitama).

fluctuated constantly and declined more sharply than rice prices whenever general economic conditions worsened. The profits tenants hoped to make proved difficult to come by. In turn, they became increasingly aware of the great advantage landlords enjoyed in selling rice, and their resentment of high rents—which prevented them, too, from participating actively in the rice market—deepened.

More conscious of the ways in which their own interests differed from those of landlords, some tenants formed associations among themselves in the late 1890s and early 1900s to promote the study of farming and to plan agricultural improvements on their own.[93] While these early tenant associations, more like friendly societies than unions, posed no immediate threat to landlords, they gave tenants experience in cooperative action and provided a basis for the more militant tenant movement of the 1920s.

Thus, as the result of agricultural improvements, the vertical ties between landlords and their tenants began to be replaced by horizontal ties among tenants themselves. No longer as dependent on their landlords' benevolence as they had been in the past, tenants had less reason to tolerate high rents. But although these checks on landlord-tenant conflict were weakened, they were by no means destroyed. Lacking alternative employment, most tenants still could not afford to offend those who provided them with land, especially when there were other cultivators eager to replace them. Even though social contact with landlords had been reduced, the very presence of landlords in the villages still militated against the open expression of conflict. These remaining barriers did not survive for long, however, in some regions of the country.

93. Ibid., p. 124.

CHAPTER FOUR

Changes in the Landlords' Role in Rural Society

Three new trends among Japanese landlords became apparent after the turn of the twentieth century. One was the steady decrease in the number of landlords who cultivated part of their holdings themselves. A second was the growing involvement of landlords in non-agricultural affairs, indicated by their declining interest in acquiring land and their greater investment in industry and commerce. A third was the gradual increase in absentee ownership. Although none of these trends can be documented rigorously, the fragmentary evidence that is available suggests that all three trends were more pronounced in economically advanced regions like the Kinki than in backward regions like the Tohoku.

The Decline of the Cultivating Landlord

As noted previously, one may divide landlords into two general categories, those who cultivated a substantial part of their holdings themselves, typically using hired labor, and derived most of their income from farming rather than rents, and those who cultivated little, if any, of their own land, leasing the greater part to tenants and living off rents. It is generally agreed that the former—the so-called cultivating landlords—were common, if not in the majority, during early Meiji.[1]

1. Ronald Dore, "The Meiji Landlord: Good or Bad?," *Journal of Asian Studies*

According to data collected by the government in 1874, farm laborers—and by extension, the landlords who hired them to cultivate their holdings—were found in every prefecture.[2] In one village in Nagano Prefecture in the same year, three out of four owners of over 5 *chō* of land farmed at least 3 *chō*.[3] Six old farmers interviewed in the 1930s about conditions in their native villages (in Hyogo, Ishikawa, Tochigi, Fukushima, Nagano, and Toyama Prefectures) reported that landlord cultivation was actually more common than tenancy in the early Meiji period.[4] There were, of course, some landlords who farmed no land at all, chiefly among merchants who had acquired land during the late Tokugawa period or shortly after the Restoration and among landlords in the cotton-producing regions of Osaka and in other regions where commercial farming had developed.[5]

At any rate, cultivating landlords still existed in sufficient number in early Meiji for their subsequent decline—in the 1890s and thereafter—to be reported by contemporary observers as a significant change in farm management. In 1901, for example, an agricultural association in Hyogo Prefecture reported:

Wages for agricultural labor have increased in recent years because of the general rise in prices and the development of commerce and industry. In the past ten years they have almost trebled. Working conditions have also improved. Treated as slaves in the past, workers are now treated as guests. . . . At present, wages amount to 50 yen a year; adding food and other expenses, they total 90 yen. Because a worker labors only about 250 days a year, that works out to 36 sen a day. Using this kind of labor, however, it is no longer possible to grow rice at a profit. Many farmers have therefore reduced the area of land they cultivate and the number of workers they employ. . . . None of the landlords in the village has given up farming completely, but most try to provide the necessary labor themselves . . . and cultivate only a very small area.[6]

---

18 (May 1959): 350; Yamaguchi Kazuo, *Meiji zenki keizai no bunseki* (Tokyo, 1956), p. 60.

2. Ibid., p. 58.

3. Ibid., p. 59.

4. Ibid.

5. Ibid., pp. 59–60

6. Watanabe Shin'ichi, "Rōdō ichiba no hatten to kosaku kankei," *Nōgyō to keizai* 4:1 (1937): 14–15.

Somewhat later, similar reports were made in the Tohoku. Officials in Aomori Prefecture observed in 1912 that:

Since the mid-1890s many local residents have moved to Hokkaido. As a result, wages for farm workers have risen, and many landlords have abandoned farming in recent years.[7]

In 1934 the Ministry of Agriculture noted the following about conditions in Iwate Prefecture:

Since the middle of the Meiji period feudalistic master-servant relations between landlords and tenants . . . have gradually weakened. The number of *nago* has decreased greatly. In order to maintain cultivation of their own land, landlords have had to rely on wage labor. Wages, however, have risen steeply, creating an imbalance between income and expenditure. As a result, landlords who once cultivated large holdings are gradually giving up farming.[8]

As these reports indicate, shortages of farm laborers and a consequent increase in their wages were an important reason why landlords were abandoning farming. Throughout most of the country in the mid-1880s the only occupations which paid less than that of farm laborer were manservant and maid. A laborer in a sake brewery in Fukushima Prefecture in 1884 earned more than twice as much as a farm laborer per year.[9] The average monthly wages of female textile workers in 1885 were roughly two and one-half times the monthly wages of female farm workers.[10] It is not surprising, then, that many daughters and younger sons of farm families, precisely that group which in the past had formed the agricultural hired labor force,[11] left their native villages during the Meiji period to work in expanding urban industries or to colonize new land in Hokkaido.

By the end of the Meiji period, in response to labor shortages in rural areas, wages for farm workers in most prefectures were two or even three times higher than they had been in the 1890s.[12] On the whole, however, increases in rice prices during the same period kept pace with these wage increases. If a landlord was willing to pay the

7. Ibid., p. 15.
9. Ibid., p. 63 (Table 4).
11. Ibid., pp. 74–75.
8. Yamaguchi, *Keizai no bunseki,* p. 74.
10. Ibid. (Table 5).
12. Ibid., p. 76 (Table 20).

higher wages necessary to attract workers, he could still make a profit from farming.[13] But other factors made it even more profit- able to lease land to tenants. The growth of industrial employment opportunities and the opening of new land were sufficient to absorb the surplus natural increase of the farm population, but not enough to upset the unfavorable ratio between population and land which existed in rural Japan. As in the past, tenants were willing to pay high rents in kind to cultivate additional land.[14] By leasing rather than cultivating their land, landlords not only avoided labor costs but also rising costs for fertilizers and tools, making a greater profit than cultivating landlords. One hypothetical example, based on conditions in Tokyo Prefecture in 1897, is given in Table 4. The landlord who leased his land and received half the crop as rent made a profit of 6 yen per *tan*, 1.20 yen per *tan* more than the land- lord who hired workers to cultivate the same area.

A final factor inducing landlords to abandon farming was the diminished risk of leasing land. One important reason for landlord cultivation in early Meiji was the insecurity of farming. Given the frequency of crop failures and the custom of reducing or canceling rents at such times, a landlord who leased his entire holding might in some years receive little, if any, income. To guarantee his own

---

13. Given the nature of wet rice cultivation, human labor could not easily be replaced by draft animals or machines. Ronald Dore, *Land Reform in Japan* (London, 1959), p. 18; Yamaguchi, *Keizai no bunseki,* p. 76. Yamaguchi cites as an exceptional case the Nakai of Tottori Prefecture, who farmed 5.8 *chō* in 1904 with the help of four workers hired on an annual basis and a number of day laborers hired to assist at planting and harvest times. Owing to the advanced farming techniques the Nakai employed (including the use of draft animals and a mechanical weeder invented by a member of the family, as well as large quantities of fertilizer) and close supervision of their laborers (whose wages appear to have been lower than usual in the area), they achieved yields of 2.7 *koku* per *tan* on their 3.6 *chō* of paddy when average yields throughout the nation were only 1.6 *koku* per *tan*. As a result, they made a net profit of over 800 yen on their rice crop, 210 yen more than they would have earned if they had leased their paddy to tenants at prevailing rents. If they had achieved only normal yields, however, they would have made a profit of 312 yen, 24 yen less than they would have earned from the tenant rents. Had they found it necessary to pay average or higher than average wages to their workers, their profits from farming would have been reduced accordingly. Ibid., pp. 64–71.

14. Dore, *Land Reform,* pp. 17–18.

TABLE 4.
A Comparison of the Profit per Tan *of
Cultivating and Non-Cultivating Landlords*

A. The cultivating landlord, using hired labor

Income

sale of rice (2 *koku*)	18.00	
sale of straw	1.40	
sale of chaff	.15	
		19.55 yen

Expenses

fertilizer	4.00	
seeds	.25	
labor	7.00	
tools	.50	
taxes	3.00	
		14.75 yen
Net profit		4.80 yen

B. The non-cultivating landlord

Income (1 *koku* of rent)	9.00 yen
Expenses (taxes)	3.00 yen
Net profit	6.00 yen

Source: Taguchi Fukichi, "Kome no keizai," *Nihon nōgyō hattatsu shi* 1: 94–95, quoted in Yamaguchi Kazuo, *Meiji zenki keizai no bunseki* (Tokyo, 1956), p. 80 (Table 27).

food supply and his ability to pay taxes, he was motivated to farm at least a few *tan* himself. By late Meiji, however, although custom still demanded that landlords reduce rents when harvests were poor, crop failures were less frequent, owing in large measure to improvements in flood control and the widespread use of hardier strains of rice. Even in remote regions, then, where wages for farm workers generally did not increase as much as in industrial regions, landlords were inclined to abandon farming or to reduce the area of land they cultivated.[15]

A rough idea of the extent to which landlords abandoned farming can be obtained from the statistics on land ownership and farm households collected by the government after 1908 (Table 5).[16] In 1908, for example, 46 percent of all landowners owning 3 *chō* or

TABLE 5.
Non-Cultivating Landlords, 1908–1927
(excluding Hokkaido and Okinawa)

	1908	1927
Owners 3 *chō* or more (A)	358,110 (100%)	308,068 (100%)
Cultivators 3 *chō* or more (B)	166,427 (46.5%)	104,905 (34.0%)
Non-cultivating landlords (A - B)	191,683 (53.5%)	203,163 (66.0%)
Owners 5 *chō* or more (C)	130,614 (100%)	111,679 (100%)
Cultivators 5 *chō* or more (D)	41,642 (31.9%)	15,994 (14.3%)
Non-cultivating landlords (C - D)	88,972 (68.1%)	95,685 (85.7%)

Source: Chūō bukka tōsei kyōryoku kaigi, *Nihon ni okeru nōgyō keiei narabi ni tochi shoyū no hensen ni kansuru sankō shiryō* (Tokyo, 1943), pp. 20-21, 26-29 (Tables 3-5, 3-6, 4-5, 4-6, 4-7, 4-8).

15. See, for example, Sunaga Shigemitsu, ed., *Kindai Nihon no jinushi to nōmin* (Tokyo, 1966) pp. 164-66; Oikawa Shirō, ed., *Yamagata ken nōchi kaikaku shi* (Yamagata, 1953), p. 73.

16. I have used here and in Table 6 the same method of approximation employed by Yamaguchi, *Keizai no bunseki,* pp. 82-85: subtract the number of farm households cultivating a given area of land from the number of owners of the same area of land to yield the number of "non-cultivating landlords"—that is, those who did not cultivate *all* the land they owned. Included in the number of non-cultivating landlords, of course, are an unknown number who actually did cultivate land, anywhere from a few *tan* to just slightly less than the full amount they owned. I should also note that Yamaguchi's method of determining the number of non-cultivating landlords differs from that used in Table 1. Figures are readily available for the number of landowners by size of holding, but no data exist for the number of landowning farmers (owner-cultivators and part-tenants) by area of land owned. Therefore, if one wants to assess the withdrawal from farming of landlords of a certain size, one must employ figures for farm households, which include landless tenants as well as owner-cultivators and part-tenants. It is unlikely, however, that many landless tenants cultivated as much as 3 *chō* of land.

more appear to have cultivated at least that much themselves; 54 percent were non-cultivating landlords, some farming less than 3 *chō* and others farming no land at all. Only 32 percent of landowners owning 5 *chō* or more cultivated at least that amount themselves; 68 percent were non-cultivating landlords. By 1927 the percentage of non-cultivating landlords had increased to 66 percent of all owners of 3 *chō* or more of land and to 86 percent of all owners of 5 *chō* or more.

Regional differences were pronounced (Table 6). In the Tohoku, non-cultivating landlords accounted for only 42 percent of all landowners owing 5 *chō* or more in 1908. In the Kinki, however, 87 percent of all owners of 5 *chō* or more were non-cultivating landlords. By 1927 the percentage of non-cultivating landlords in both districts had increased—to 71 percent in the Tohoku and 98 percent in the Kinki.[17]

The Growing Involvement of Landlords in Non-Agricultural Affairs

As noted previously, the extent of tenanted land increased from 36 percent of all arable land in 1883 to 45 percent in 1908.[18] Part of this increase was caused by the landlords' abandonment of farming; that is, land which they had once farmed themselves and which had been recorded as owner-cultivated land was now recorded as tenanted land.[19] Part may also have been caused by the registration of previously concealed tenanted land, typically in the aftermath of land adjustment projects. But in many parts of the country, the

17. One should remember, of course, that the figures given in Table 6, like those in Table 5, are rough approximations, which exaggerate the extent of the landlords' abandonment of farming: an unknown number of "non-cultivating landlords" in both the Tohoku and the Kinki still farmed some portion of their land themselves.

18. See Araki Moriaki, "Jinushi sei no tenkai," in *Iwanami kōza Nihon rekishi* 16 (Tokyo, 1962): 74 (Table 2-14) for the extent of tenanted land by prefecture, 1883–1908. Furushima employs slightly different, and probably more accurate, figures for 1883. See Furushima Toshio, ed., *Nihon jinushi sei shi kenkyū* (Tokyo, 1958), p. 331, for a brief discussion of the different estimates of tenanted land in the early 1880s.

19. Oda Matatarō, "Jinushi to kosakunin ni tsuite ichigen," *Dai Nippon nōkai hō*, No. 187 (1897), quoted in Yamaguchi, *Keizai no bunseki,* pp. 72–73.

TABLE 6.
Non-Cultivating Landlords in the Tohoku and Kinki,
1908–1927

Year	Tohoku	Kinki
1908		
Owners 5 *chō* or more (C)	21,911 (100%)	7,951 (100%)
Cultivators 5 *chō* or more (D)	12,692 (57.9%)	1,000 (12.6%)
Non-cultivating landlords (C - D)	9,219 (42.1%)	6,951 (87.4%)
1927		
Owners 5 *chō* or more (C)	21,438 (100%)	6,641 (100%)
Cultivators 5 *chō* or more (D)	6,205 (29.0%)	141 (2.1%)
Non-cultivating landlords (C - D)	15,233 (71.0%)	6,500 (97.9%)

Source: See Table 4.

most substantial increases in the extent of tenanted land occurred between 1883 and 1887 (Table 7). Since it was not until later that many landlords withdrew from farming or that much concealed land was uncovered by adjustment, one can assume that these earlier increases were largely the result of actual transfers of ownership—the expansion of existing landlord holdings and the creation of new ones.

It was during the 1880s that the effects of the Matsukata deflation, begun in 1881, were most keenly felt in rural areas. As rice prices fell, causing an increase in the burden of the land tax, many landowners went into debt or were unable to pay existing debts. Between 1884 and 1886 the value of land foreclosed by lenders amounted to over 8 percent of total land values.[20] Roughly 47,000 *chō* were auctioned off for tax arrears between 1883 and 1889, sold at low prices to anyone with cash on hand.[21] The number of men

20. Saitō Eiichi, "Jinushi no zaisan kōsei ni tsuite," part 1, *Shakai seisaku jihō*, No. 156 (September 1933), pp. 72–73.
21. Ibid., pp. 70–71.

73

TABLE 7.

The Timing of Increases in the Extent of Tenanted Land,
1883–1908

Years	Number of prefectures with greatest increase between 1883 and 1908	Number of prefectures with smallest increase between 1883 and 1908
1883–1887	20	4
1887–1892	5	17
1892–1903	14	9
1903–1908	2	11
Total	41	Total 41

Source: Araki Moriaki, "Jinushi sei no tenkai," in *Iwanami kōza Nihon rekishi* 16 (Tokyo, 1962): 76 (Table 2-17).

qualified to stand for election to prefectural assemblies (roughly equivalent to the owners of over 1.6 *chō* of land) declined by 14 percent between 1881 and 1890. In the same period, however, individuals qualified only to vote in prefectural elections (roughly equivalent to the owners of 0.8 to 1.6 *chō*) declined by 30 percent.[22] These data suggest that larger landowners had less trouble than their smaller counterparts in withstanding the effects of the deflation.

Hirata Yasukichi, the Yamagata landlord mentioned previously, was able to acquire 9 *chō* within the city limits of Tsuruoka in the late 1880s, when it was said by local residents that anyone with money to buy a piece of *tōfu* (bean-curd) could buy a plot of land instead. Converting the land into dry fields, he raised soybeans and planted apple and peach trees, from which he later realized a good profit.[23]

Although the data on which he based his observation were lost during the Kanto earthquake of 1923, Kobayashi Heizaemon re-

22. Araki, "Jinushi sei," p. 78 (Table 2-19).
23. In addition to severe depression, the city of Tsuruoka was also ravaged by a fire in 1888. Koyama Magojirō, "Meiji ni okeru jinushi no nōji kairyō undō," in Nōgyō hattatsu shi chōsa kai, ed., *Nihon nōgyō hattatsu shi* 5: 605–6.

called that of over one hundred large landlords he interviewed in the early 1920s, the majority had acquired most of their land between 1884 and 1889.[24] As Fukuzawa Yukichi remarked in mid-Meiji, "Every year the number of people losing land increases, and the trend toward the concentration of land in the hands of wealthy men grows more pronounced."[25]

Yet after the turn of the century the trend toward increasing tenancy slackened. The area of tenanted land rose from 45 percent of arable land in 1908 to only 46 percent in 1941 (though of a considerably larger acreage).[26] From government surveys of land ownership, it appears that owners of over 10 *chō* of land increased in number through 1923, but since we have no way of knowing how much land these owners possessed at any time, we cannot determine if their individual holdings increased in size or not.[27] On the basis of specific case histories, however, it appears that even when landlords did expand their holdings after the turn of the century, the rate of expansion was much less than before. The Itō of Niigata Prefecture, for example, acquired 282 *chō* between 1907 and 1924,

24. Ono Takeo, *Nōson shi,* vol. 9 of *Gendai Nihon bunmei shi* (Tokyo, 1941), p. 67, note 1. Kobayashi confined his survey to landlords owning 10 *chō* or more.
25. Fukuzawa Yukichi, *Fukuzawa zenshū* 4: 382, quoted in Saitō, "Zaisan kōsei," part 1, p. 67.
26. Dore, *Land Reform,* p. 19.
27. The statistics compiled annually by the Ministry of Agriculture divide landowners into seven categories according to the size of their holdings: less than 5 *tan,* from 5 *tan* to less than 1 *chō,* 1 to less than 3 *chō,* 3 to less than 5 *chō,* 5 to less than 10 *chō,* 10 to less than 50 *chō,* and 50 *chō* or more. But only the number of landowners is given for each category, not the total area of land they owned. As a result, one can only estimate the upper and lower limits of acreage for the second through the sixth categories. That is, if 900,000 landowners are listed for the third category, 1 to less than 3 *chō,* one can say that they owned at least 900,000 but no more than 2,700,000 *chō.* For the two categories at either end of the scale, less than 5 *tan* and 50 *chō* or more, no such calculation is possible. This situation makes it virtually impossible to analyze historical changes in land ownership—in particular, the subject of the concentration of land ownership. Tōbata Seiichi, *Nōchi o meguru jinushi to nōmin* (Tokyo, 1947), pp. 13–15. Some scholars have attempted to assess the concentration of land ownership by multiplying the number of landowners in each category by the average area of the category (by 2 *chō* for the category 1–3 *chō,* etc.). For one such attempt, which indicates that the holdings of large landlords did increase in size through 1923, see Takahashi Kamekichi, *Meiji Taishō nōson no hensen* (Tokyo, 1926), pp. 91–96.

an increase of roughly 17 *chō* per year. But between 1868 and 1907 they had acquired 1,043 *chō,* or almost 27 *chō* per year.[28]

There are a number of reasons for this apparent decline in the accumulation of land. In the first place, land was more difficult to acquire. Not only had land prices risen, but also, with the increased security of farming and gradual development of rural credit associations,[29] opportunities to gain control of land by means of foreclosure had diminished. Of more importance, however, in explaining why landlords acquired less land after the turn of the century was the increasing attractiveness of other forms of investment.

In the Meiji period land was clearly the most secure, if not the most profitable, investment. High rents, rising rice prices (except during the depression), and a fairly stable tax burden guaranteed landlords a good income. The one major risk they faced was crop failure. In contrast, investment in industry was very risky, and profits far from certain.[30] By the Taishō period, however, the situation was reversed; investment in industry and commerce had become, since the Russo-Japanese War, more profitable than investment in land. If, for example, an individual purchased 10 *chō* of land in the early 1920s and let it to tenants at average rents, his net income after taxes would amount to 5.3 percent of the price of the land. Had he purchased shares of stock in the Kanegafuchi textile company instead, he would receive a net return of 10.8 percent on his investment, roughly twice as much. Moreover, as a landlord he would pay 11.3 percent of his gross income in direct taxes. As a businessman with the same income he would pay only 3.9 percent; as an investor, only 0.1 percent.[31]

28. Interview with Kubo Yasuo.

29. Tōbata Seiichi, "Nihon nōgyō hatten no ninaite," in *Nōgyō* hattatsu shi chōsa kai, ed., *Nihon nōgyō hattatsu shi* 9: 588.

30. For one example of the risks in industry, see Denda Isao, "Kokuminshugi shisō to nōhonshugi shisō," in *Meiji zenhan ki no nashonarizumu,* ed. Sakata Yoshio (Tokyo, 1958), pp. 268–71.

31. Dorothy Orchard, "Agrarian Problems of Modern Japan," *Journal of Political Economy* 37 (April 1929): 131–36; Saitō, "Jinushi no zaisan kōsei ni tsuite," part 2, *Shakai seisaku jihō,* No. 157 (October 1933), p. 74.

There are, unfortunately, no comprehensive surveys of landlord investment outside the agricultural sector. But available data, while fragmentary, suggest that the involvement of landlords in non-agricultural enterprises, principally as investors but also as entrepreneurs and managers, increased after the turn of the century.

It was, of course, not a totally new phenomenon. Hirata Yasukichi began a number of enterprises in the 1880s and 1890s, among them a dairy, a transportation business, and a silk mill. In 1895, to challenge the economic power of the Sakai family and other former members of the domain aristocracy, he helped organize both the Tsuruoka Rice Exchange and a bank to support its activities.[32] Landlords generally were active in banking during early and mid-Meiji, especially in regions where cash crops were grown.[33] In addition, some 20 percent of subscriptions to domestic long-term bonds were purchased by large landlords between 1868 and 1893.[34]

How many landlords started commercial and industrial enterprises or invested in stocks and bonds at this time is, of course, not known, but the evidence suggests that the degree of participation in non-agricultural economic development did not satisfy the Meiji government. In 1876, for example, Ōkubo Toshimichi had personally urged the Homma family, the largest landlords in Japan, to establish a silk mill, apparently failing to persuade them.[35] Other government officials reported similar failures.[36] In 1884 the Ministry of Agriculture and Commerce observed that of the products manufactured by landlords and rural merchants in the late 1870s, "most (80-90 percent) are luxuries, imitating foreign products and mostly

32. Koyama, "Nōji kairyō undō," pp. 607-9.

33. James Nakamura, *Agricultural Production and the Economic Development of Japan, 1873–1922* (Princeton, 1966), pp. 166-69.

34. Ibid., p. 169. See also G. Ranis, "Financing of Japanese Economic Development," *Economic History Review* 9 (April 1959): 447, 450; Morita Shirō, *Jinushi keizai to chihō shihon* (Tokyo, 1963), especially chapters II and III.

35. Denda, "Kokuminshugi shisō," pp. 264-65, note 2.

36. Kazushi Ohkawa and Henry Rosovsky, "A Century of Japanese Economic Growth," in *The State and Economic Enterprise in Japan,* ed. William Lockwood (Princeton, 1965), p. 65.

made of imported materials. The manufacture of these contributed little to increase national power."[37]

The situation began to change, however, in the 1890s. Increased economic stability and the completion of legal codes governing business transactions helped overcome the landlords' reluctance to invest outside agriculture. Second, the granting of political rights in the 1880s and the opening of the Diet in 1890 increased the familiarity of landlords with national economic affairs.

Roughly half of the members of the lower house of the Diet during its first six sessions listed their occupations as "farmer" or "landlord."[38] Landlords were also among the forty-five members elected from—and by—the nation's highest taxpayers to the House of Peers. In 1890 almost half of the tax peers listed their occupation as farming. Among the others were many men who, whatever their listed occupations, owned at least 50 *chō* of land.[39] Flattered by admission to national politics, these landlords became more receptive to the urgings of government officials that they participate actively in the country's economic development. Merely being in Tokyo, an important commercial center as well as the capital city, they learned how they could profit from industrial development. Ishijima Tokujirō, for example, owner of over 1,000 *chō* in Niigata, first heard about the stock market while attending the Diet session in 1890 as a tax peer. Thereafter, he maintained a program of regular investment. By 1907 dividends from stocks amounted to 13 percent of his total income; by 1925, to 22 percent. In 1928 almost half his property was in stocks and bonds.[40]

The Hoshijima, owners of over 200 *chō* and among the highest taxpayers in Okayama Prefecture, stopped accumulating arable land in 1895. They began investing in the stock market in 1887, purchasing most of their holdings after 1894. Their purchases totaled 336,702 yen in 1906—roughly 65 percent in national rail-

37. Ibid., pp. 64-65.
38. Araki, "Jinushi sei," pp. 98-99.
39. Ibid., pp. 100-101.
40. Interview with Kubo Yasuo; Nōchi kaikaku kiroku iinkai, ed., *Nōchi kaikaku tenmatsu gaiyō* (Tokyo, 1951), p. 819 (Table A).

roads, 24 percent in local industries, 5 percent each in bonds and national industries, and 1 percent in local railroads.[41]

The Fujita family, also of Okayama Prefecture, owned 88 *chō* of land and 2,740 yen of stocks and bonds in 1887. Their total yearly income was 1,230 yen—66.6 percent from tenant rents, 18.3 percent from loans, 11.7 percent from dividends, and 3.4 percent from house rentals. By 1904 they owned 332,832 yen of stocks and bonds—roughly 59 percent in government securities, 32 percent in local and national enterprises, and 9 percent in banks. In 1926 they owned slightly more than 100 *chō* of land and received only 52 percent of their income from tenant rents; 23.3 percent, roughly double the percentage in 1887, was derived from dividends. House rentals accounted for 21.3 percent of income, and salaries (from the family head's positions with a local bank and railroad) to 3.4 percent.[42]

The Tamaki, owners of over 670 *chō* in Niigata Prefecture in 1924, not only ceased acquiring land in the early 1900s but also began selling off substantial portions of their holdings. In part this was because the head of the family had been warned by a fortune-teller of some repute that trouble lay ahead for landlords: they would have problems with their tenants and eventually would lose their land. Even earlier, however, the family head had begun to keep detailed records of his income and expenses, employing up-to-date bookkeeping methods he had learned as a student of political economy at Waseda University. He had concluded that his land holdings represented an insufficiently rewarding investment. Rather than maintain the large staff required to manage his land, he preferred to sell as much as he could and invest the proceeds in non-agricultural enterprises.[43]

Although the evidence is far from conclusive, it appears probable

41. Ota Ken'ichi, "Setōnaikai engan chiiki ni okeru jinushi sei no dōkō," *Tochi seido shigaku,* No. 27, pp. 63-66 (Tables 9, 12).

42. Ota Ken'ichi, "Fujita ke no sonzai keitai," *Jinya machi no kenkyū* (Okayama, n.d.), pp. 171-77.

43. Interview with Tamaki Hisako, village official and former landlord, Tagami, Minamikambara *gun,* Niigata Prefecture, 11 August 1967.

that the shift away from investment in land to investment outside
the agricultural sector among large landlords such as those cited
above was greatest in the most economically advanced regions of
the country. Over half the landlords owning 50 *chō* or more in the
Kinki and Chugoku districts who were listed by name in the registers
of large landlords compiled in 1890 and 1898[44] were not included in
the register of 1924.[45] Some had been forced to sell all or part of
their land to cover business losses, while others had done so voluntarily, to generate capital for industrial investment. In the Tohoku
district, however, less than one-third of the landlords owning 50 *chō*
or more in the 1890s were not included in the 1924 register, an
"attrition rate" significantly less than the national average of 38
percent.[46]

Information on the non-agricultural investments of smaller landlords is scarce, but since they were by no means wealthy—in the
1930s a holding of 5 to 6 *chō* was needed to provide an income from
rents equivalent to the salary of an urban civil servant or teacher[47]—
it seems reasonable to conclude that they did not invest as regularly
or, proportionate to their incomes, as heavily as large landlords.[48]
That does not mean, however, that they remained intimately involved in agricultural affairs. On the contrary, their inability to
make a comfortable living from leasing land alone induced many
smaller landlords to seek additional sources of income. Some continued as part-time farmers, but many obtained employment outside

44. Itō Masagi, ed., *Dai Nippon tagaku nōzeisha meibo* (Niigata, 1890) and
Suzuki Kihachi and Seki Itarō, eds., *Nihon zenkoku shōkōjin meibo* (1898),
described and analyzed in Shibutani Ryūichi and Ishiyama Shōjirō, "Meiji chūki
no jinushi meibo," *Tochi seido shigaku*, No. 30 (June 1966), pp. 54-57.

45. Nōrinshō, nōmukyoku, "Gojitchōbu ijō no ōjinushi meibo (1924)," in *Nihon
nōgyō hattatsu shi* 9: 705-74. The Chugoku consists of Okayama, Hiroshima,
Yamaguchi, Shimane, and Tottori Prefectures.

46. Shibutani and Ishiyama, "Meiji chūki no jinushi meibo," p. 58.

47. Dore, *Land Reform*, p. 29; Tōbata Seiichi, *Nihon shihonshugi no keisei sha*
(Tokyo, 1964), p. 133.

48. See *Nōchi kaikaku tenmatsu gaiyō*, p. 809 (Table 3), for data on the sources
of income for landlords owning from 10 to over 100 *chō* in Niigata Prefecture in
1935. The "smaller" of these landlords, who owned between 10 and 20 *chō*, derived
only 6.2 percent of their incomes from stocks; those with over 100 *chō* derived
70.2 percent.

the communities in which they lived, in banks, businesses or government offices in nearby towns and cities.[49] The opportunities for such employment were greater, one can assume, in the more economically advanced and urbanized parts of the country than in the relatively undeveloped hinterland.

Absentee Landlords

Absentee ownership was not an entirely new phenomenon in rural Japan. Many large holdings in the Shōnai plain of Yamagata Prefecture during the late Tokugawa period, for example, were owned by landlord-merchants living in Sakata and Tsuruoka. Typically, landlords who financed reclamation projects before the Restoration were also absentee owners, living some distance away from their new holdings.[50] But it appears that absentee ownership began to increase in late Meiji.

In part this was simply the result of the expansion of landlord holdings. Even though an individual might himself remain in one place, as soon as he acquired land in another village or *gun,* he became, in a geographical sense, an absentee owner. And, in part, the increase in absentee ownership was the result of new land reclamation projects and of new purchases of land by urban businessmen—that is, of the continuation of trends which had existed in the past as well. But a new trend was also visible—the movement of resident landlords from their native villages to the cities.

One reason for their departure was the growing burden of local taxes, especially the *kosūwari,* or house tax. The *kosūwari* was a tax levied by cities, towns, and villages (and indirectly by prefectures, on the basis of the amount paid in the above administrative units) on the income and property of households or of any person living independently. In pure farming villages, those with no shops or

49. Tōbata, *Nihon shihonshugi no keisei sha,* p. 133. Those who worked for the government as teachers, policemen, or agricultural advisers were required by law to work outside the communities of their birth.

50. For examples from Okayama Prefecture, see James A. Kokoris, "The Ohara Zaibatsu of Okayama," University of Michigan Center for Japanese Studies, *Occasional Papers,* No. 8 (1964), p. 40.

businesses, where there was little taxable wealth other than land, buildings, and agricultural income, it amounted to an additional land and income surtax.[51]

In 1908 the Diet established legal limits for local surtaxes on land and income,[52] but no limits were established for the *kosūwari*. In response to increased local expenses after the turn of the century—for school construction and the expansion of public services, for example—it soon became the most important source of revenue at the town and village level. As shown in Table 8, house taxes more than doubled between 1900 and 1909.

As a rule, the *kosūwari* was only levied on actual residents of a city, town, or village. In cities, especially in large cities with many other sources of revenue, it was not very high. Sometimes city residents were required to pay taxes on property they held elsewhere, but this was generally not the case. Typically, their tax was determined solely by the size of their current residence or, alternatively, by its rental value.[53] Thus a landlord who moved from his native village, where the *kosūwari* was high, to a city, where it was low, would be able to reduce his tax burden (and increase his profits) considerably.

The taxes paid in 1915 by two resident landlords in a village in Osaka Prefecture are listed in Table 9. Landlord A owned 11 *chō* of paddy, 6 *chō* of dry fields, 1 *chō* of residential land, and 2 *chō* of forest and waste land, for a total of 20 *chō*, valued for tax purposes at 8,400 yen. Landlord B owned 1.3 *chō* of paddy and 1.4 *chō* of dry fields, for a total of 2.7 *chō*, valued at 1,300 yen. Both holdings

51. Higashiura Shōji, "Mura no zaisei to fuzai jinushi ni tsuite no jirei hitotsu," *Teikoku nōkai hō* 15 (February 1925): 7. See also Takahashi, *Nōson keizai no hensen*, pp. 35–36, where the author presents a table indicating that the net income of landlords rose by over 600 percent between 1885 and 1925, owing chiefly to increases in rice prices. His table, frequently cited in studies of landlords, includes as expenses only the national land tax and local land surtax, not the income tax or the *kosūwari*. The latter was a particularly crucial omission.

52. Higashiura, "Mura no zaisei," p. 7. For rates of national and local taxes between 1873 and 1915 see Ogura Takekazu, *Tochi rippō no shiteki kōsatsu* (Tokyo, 1951), p. 129, note 9; Toyama Shinzō, "Fuzai jinushi to kazei," *Teikoku nōkai hō* 6 (October 1916): 36.

53. Ibid., pp. 36–38.

TABLE 8.
Increases in House Taxes, 1900–1909
(in 1,000's of yen)

	1900	1909	Rate of increase
Local taxes on land			
prefectural	21,938	24,849	13.3%
city, town, and village	12,051	13,434	11.5%
Total	33,989	38,283	12.6%
House taxes			
prefectural	7,896	12,243	55%
city, town, and village	23,691	54,474	130%
Total	31,587	66,717	111%

Source: Toyama Shinzō, "Fuzai jinushi to kazei," *Teikoku nōkai hō* 6 (October 1916): 37.

were located within the village boundaries, and both landlords derived almost all of their income from leasing land.[54] If Landlord A left the village, he would not have to pay 143 yen in village house taxes; he would probably also avoid the prefectural house tax of 26 yen since it was usually collected by the village office. Similarly, Landlord B, by becoming an absentee landlord, would not have to pay 23 yen in house taxes.

In 1903 the house taxes levied in Niikura village in Saitama Prefecture totaled 251 yen, 14 percent of the village land surtax. By 1921 house taxes had risen to 7,950 yen and were four times greater than village land surtaxes. Resident households, owning a total of 245 *chō* of land, paid a total of 9,235 yen in village taxes, an average of 3.76 yen per *tan* of land they owned. In contrast, non-resident landowners, who owned 81 *chō* of village land, paid only 765.9 yen in village taxes, an average of .945 yen per *tan* of land

54. Ibid., p. 37.

TABLE 9.
Taxes Paid by Two Landlords in Osaka, 1915
(in yen)

Taxes	Landlord A		Landlord B	
Land tax		369.28		53.95
Land surtax				
prefectural	110.73		15.55	
village	72.81		10.23	
		183.54		25.78
Public imposts				
irrigation	43.43		5.36	
agricultural association	17.23		2.27	
		60.66		7.63
Income tax		61.64		----
Income surtax				
prefectural	2.44		----	
village	9.22		----	
		11.66		----
House tax				
prefectural	26.32		3.59	
village	142.92		19.53	
		169.24		23.12
Total		856.02		110.48

Source: Toyama Shinzō, "Fuzai jinushi to kazei," *Teikoku nōkai hō* 6 (October 1916): 37.

owned. One landlord owning 10 *chō* of land but residing in Tokyo paid only 55 yen in village taxes. A village landlord with a similar holding paid 266 yen.[55]

55. Higashiura, "Mura no zaisei," pp. 6–8. The house tax the absentee landlord paid in Tokyo was probably much less than he would have paid in the village.

Although difficult to document, there were a number of other reasons in addition to the burden of local taxes which induced landlords to leave their native villages. All of them can best be summarized as a growing dissatisfaction with rural life. A landlord who had grown up since the Restoration reading Samuel Smiles's *Self-Help* (translated into Japanese in 1871 and an immediate best-seller) and hearing about the accomplishments of famous entre-preneurs might easily feel that he was isolated from the mainstream of national life and unable to put his own talent and capital to good use as long as he remained, so to speak, "on the farm."[56] Or he might wish to lead the more cultured life (*bunka seikatsu*) of a city dweller, attending plays, dining on beef or other exotic foods, and enjoying such modern wonders as electricity and a telephone in his own home.[57] Such comforts could, of course, be imported from cities to rural villages. Nōzaki Būkichirō, a large landlord in Okayama Prefecture, had electricity, running water, and a private phone system installed in his country home and office in the early 1900s.[58] But the expense was great; only the wealthiest landlords could afford to live as well as the urban upper classes while remaining in the countryside.

As Ronald Dore has noted, some old landed families purposely avoided educating their heirs in an attempt to insulate them from new ideas and ambitions and thereby preserve the family's status in the village. But with education as highly valued as it was in Japan, few landlords could deny their sons a higher education if they desired it. Some of these sons did return home, often to carry out reforms in farming and village administration based on the new knowledge they had acquired. But many stayed away, retaining the family land after their parents' death while working in the cities. Included in this category were a number of professors and govern-ment officials who, as absentee landlords, later participated in the

56. Toyama, "Fuzai jinushi," p. 36.
57. Mochizuki Shikazō, "Fuzei jinushi bokumetsu saku," *Nōsei kenkyū* 5: 9 (1926): 19.
58. Interview with Namba Giichirō, steward to the Nōzaki family since the early 1900s, 14 May 1967.

drafting of the postwar Land Reform Bill.[59] Still others, while studying at universities in the early 1920s, became active in the radical student movement and returned home, not to preserve the family status, but to struggle for the emancipation of tenant farmers and to urge their parents to liquidate their holdings. Miyake Seiichi, for instance, son of a well-to-do landlord, helped organize one of the largest tenancy disputes in Niigata Prefecture after his graduation from Waseda and remained an active member of the Japanese Socialist Party in the post-World War II era.[60]

Statistical data on absentee ownership in the Meiji and Taishō periods are far from comprehensive. The results of a survey conducted in nine villages throughout the country in early Taishō (Table 10) indicate that absentee ownership had increased since 1890 and that it was more common for paddy than for dry land (note, however, that the rate of increase for dry land was far greater than for paddy). In Niikura, the village in Saitama Prefecture mentioned previously, non-residents owned 25 percent of village land, including 42 percent of village paddy and 17 percent of village dry land.[61]

According to the survey of landlords owning 50 *chō* or more conducted by the Ministry of Agriculture in 1924, 4 percent of the total number (excluding Hokkaido) resided outside the prefecture in which their land was located; 26 percent resided in another *gun* or city. Only 17 percent of landlords with land in the Tohoku resided in another *gun* or city, compared to 52 percent in the Kinki.[62] Almost all large landlords, of course, owned land in several villages (a few of them in fifty or more).[63] Even if resident in the prefecture or *gun* in which their land was located, they were likely to be regarded as absentee owners in at least a few villages.

59. Dore, *Land Reform*, pp. 23–25. See also Thomas Smith, "Landlords' Sons in the Business Elite," *Economic Development and Cultural Change* 9 (October 1960): 93–108.
60. Interview with Kubo Yasuo.
61. Higashiura, "Mura no zaisei," p. 7.
62. Tōbata, *Nōchi o meguru*, pp. 38–41.
63. Nōrinshō, nōmukyoku, "Gojitchōbu ijō no kōchi o shoyū shuru ōjinushi ni kansuru chōsa (1925)," p. 702 (Table 9).

TABLE 10.
*Percentage of Land in Nine Villages
Owned by Non-Residents*

Year	Paddy	Dry
1890	14.8%	1.7%
1899	14.2	3.4
1908	15.8	3.2
1911	16.6	4.5

Source: Toyama Shinzō, "Fuzai jinushi to kazei," *Teikoku nōkai hō* 6
(October 1916): 38.

The first nationwide survey of absentee ownership was conducted
by the government in 1941. At that time 15 percent of all arable
land (excluding Hokkaido) was owned by non-residents of the town,
village, or city in which the land was located. Roughly 12 percent
of this land was still cultivated by its "absentee" owners, who
obviously lived nearby. Some 88 percent of it was tenanted, and the
tenanted land owned by absentee landlords accounted for 30 percent
of all tenanted land.[64]

As had been the case earlier in the century, these absentee owners
of tenanted land formed a very diverse group. Their holdings varied
in size from a few *tan* to several hundred *chō*. Some had never
resided in the countryside but had acquired land only as a relatively
safe investment or as a source of good quality rice and vegetables
for a restaurant or food store. Others had once lived in the communities where their land was located, and perhaps had engaged
in farming. But for a variety of reasons—to provide a better education for their children, to escape from rural unrest in the 1920s
and 1930s, or to pursue new careers—they had departed for the
cities.[65] During World War I in particular, when rice prices rose

64. *Nōchi kaikaku tenmatsu gaiyō,* pp. 782–83 (Table 6).
65. Kozei Denzō, "Fuzai jinushi no sonzai kachi ikan," *Nōsei kenkyū* 5:9 (1926):
5; Nomura Shinshichi, "Fuzai jinushi kanarazu shimo haisubekarazu," *Nōsei
kenkyū* 5:9 (1926): 24–25.

sharply, it had become possible for many smaller landlords to send their sons to secondary schools or universities, qualifying them for positions as urban "salary men." According to one source,[66] these educational opportunities and the urban migration they encouraged among landed Japanese were greatest in the Kinki district and other economically advanced regions of the country.

Effects on Landlord-Tenant Relations

The three trends discussed thus far—the landlords' abandonment of farming, their greater involvement in non-agricultural affairs, and increasing absentee ownership—have been cited, along with rice inspection, as evidence for the growing "parasitism" of Japanese landlords and, consequently, for the worsening of tenancy conditions.[67] This argument is convenient for explaining and justifying increased unrest among tenant farmers in the Taishō period, but it is not necessarily accurate. The actual effects of these new trends were more complex, benefiting tenants in some ways and damaging their interests in others.

Ireland in the eighteenth century, "the darkest chapter in the history of English landlords,"[68] has come to epitomize the evil effects of absentee ownership. The holdings of absentee landlords were divided into tiny parcels and let at higher than average rents; overseers charged tenants special fees in addition to rents for the privilege of cultivating the land they managed and revoked tenancy at the slightest provocation; farming villages remained in wretched poverty. But the effects of absentee ownership in Japan were almost exactly the opposite.

Absentee landlords usually had other sources of income and were less dependent on tenant rents than resident landlords. As a result, the rents they charged were often lower than prevailing rents and

66. Kondō Yasuo, *Mura no kōzō* (Tokyo, 1955), pp. 426–27.
67. See Dore, "Meiji Landlord," pp. 348–55.
68. G. E. Mingay, *English Landed Society in the Eighteenth Century* (London, 1963), p. 47.

rarely any higher.[69] Living at some distance from their holdings and lacking intimate knowledge of rural conditions, absentee owners were generally more willing than resident owners to meet tenant demands for rent reductions.[70] Resident landlords bought and sold land frequently; typically, the new owners raised rents when they took possession and often evicted current tenants in favor of their own. In contrast, absentee owners rarely acquired new holdings; their tenants enjoyed greater security, farming the same plots for many years in succession.[71] In general, the tenants of absentee landlords cultivated a larger area per capita than the tenants of resident landlords. According to the survey of large landlords owning 50 or more *chō* of land in 1924, for example, the tenants of absentee landlords leased an average of 5.2 *tan*; the tenants of resident landlords, an average of 4.3 *tan*.[72] Most absentee landlords employed overseers to manage their holdings, but few cases of extortion and other unfair practices are recorded.[73]

Not all the effects of absentee ownership were beneficial, however. Some absentee landlords, although themselves non-cultivators, still provided capital for the improvement of their holdings. But on the whole, absentee landlords had little knowledge of farming and little interest in financing improvements.[74] Thus, although enjoying greater security and paying lower rents, their tenants frequently were unable to carry our projects which would raise productivity and increase tenant income.

In addition, absentee ownership often posed grave problems for village finance. Unable to tax the wealth and property of non-residents by means of the *kosūwari,* many villages were forced to

69. Tōbata, *Nōchi o meguru,* pp. 43–45; Okayama ken naimubu, *Okayama ken kosaku kankō chōsa sho* (Okayama, 1924), pp. 90–91.
70. Ibid., p. 91; Tōbata, *Nōchi o meguru,* p. 43.
71. Ibid., pp. 43–44.
72. Ibid., pp. 42, 44–45 (Table 9).
73. Ibid., pp. 45–46; Wakukawa Seiyei, "The Japanese Farm Tenancy System," in *Japan's Prospect,* ed. D. G. Haring (Cambridge, Massachusetts, 1946), p. 148; *Okayama kan kosaku kankō,* pp. 87–88.
74. Kozei, "Fuzai jinushi no sonzai kachi," p. 5.

increase the burden of taxation on residents (including taxation of the personal property and homes of landless tenants) or to curtail community services. Landlords who remained in the villages and had to bear the major share of increased local taxes were less able to aid their tenants in time of need or to provide capital for farm improvements.[75]

Like the absentee landlord, the landlord who invested part of his capital in the industrial sector was not as dependent on rental income as the non-investing landlord and was generally in a better position to grant rent reductions to his tenants. Moreover, his investments often brought immediate benefits to his tenants and the local farming population. The expansion of railroads, for example, in which landlords invested heavily, brought many villages into closer contact with lucrative urban markets for their produce and made it possible for many tenants to work in nearby towns during the off-season.[76] There were indirect benefits for tenants in landlord investment as well. If, for example, landlords had not contributed to industrial development, job opportunities for the surplus rural population would have increased at a slower rate, causing greater population pressure on the land, more intense competition for land among tenants, and hence, even higher rents.[77]

Landlord cultivation had been an important avenue for the introduction of new farming techniques in the early Meiji era. In a village in Miyagi Prefecture, for example, most of the improvements adopted by local farmers—the use of horses for plowing fields, chemical fertilizers, and treadle-operated threshing machines—had first been brought to the village by cultivating landlords for use on their own farms.[78] By means of close supervision of their laborers and advanced farming techniques, some cultivating landlords had

75. Toyama, "Fuzai jinushi," p. 39.
76. J. W. Robertson Scott, *The Foundations of Japan* (London, 1922), p. 283; John Embree, *Suye Mura, A Japanese Village* (Chicago, 1946), p. 77.
77. Dore, *Land Reform*, p. 48.
78. See Sunaga, *Kindai Nihon no jinushi*, pp. 249–50.

succeeded in raising the productivity of their land well above average levels, setting an example for other farmers and helping to overcome their opposition to paddy adjustment and other reforms which upset the established pattern of farming.

By abandoning farming, the landlords' impact on the spread of agricultural improvements did indeed diminish. But it did not cease altogether. In the late 1920s, for example, non-cultivating landlords in a village in Chiba Prefecture provided the leadership and part of the capital for the improvement of two local irrigation ponds.[79] Many other landlords, whether themselves farmers or not, remained active in the work of local agricultural associations formed with official encouragement in late Meiji, helping to transmit the results of research at government experimental stations to the general farming population.[80] Or they took part in the activities of the Imperial Agricultural Association, a nationwide federation of local associations established in the early 1900s.

Whether the problems created by changes among landlords outweighed the advantages they offered tenants cannot be determined easily. What is clear, however, is that these changes made it difficult for landlords to perform their traditional role in tenancy relations and village life.

Although they might return occasionally to their native villages—to visit family graves or tend to local business—absentee landlords gradually became strangers to the other residents. At the New Year they might still gather all their tenants together for a banquet and the distribution of gifts, but what had once been a festive occasion—a time for joking and singing—became a stiff and formal affair. Now their managers took care of day-to-day matters: the selection of tenants and the drawing up of contracts, the supervision of farming, and the collection of rents. In some cases managers also handled

79. Social Science Research Institute, *The Power Structure in a Rural Community: the Case of Mutsuzawa Mura* (Tokyo, 1960), pp. 21–22. For other examples see Kamagata Isao, *Yamagata ken inasaku shi* (Tokyo, 1953), p. 219.

80. Dore, "Meiji Landlord," p. 353.

sales of rent rice; the landlords had little to do themselves but pocket the profits.[81] To their tenants, they became distant figures, unfamiliar with local customs or with the personal lives of the people who farmed their land.

Resident landlords with large holdings were also inclined to employ managers, thereby reducing personal contacts with their tenants. Ishijima Noriatsu of Niigata Prefecture, for example, who became head of his family in 1921, was only known by sight in the hamlet in which he lived.[82] More deeply involved in national politics and concerned about their industrial investments, landlords had less time to devote to local government. Moreover, it was hard for them to compartmentalize their behavior—to compete for profits on the stock exchange and still make benevolent, and often costly, gestures toward their tenants. Instead, as one writer suggests, they became increasingly impatient with the elaborate rituals of gift-giving and the many demands made upon their time and wealth. Some attempted to lease as much of their land as possible to tenants in other villages—thereby becoming absentee landlords without moving at all—to escape the personalized relations which existed in their own communities.[83]

Even those landlords who tried to perform their traditional role in rural society found after the turn of the century that many of their functions had been usurped. Through the agricultural associations to which they belonged, tenants had learned more about farming themselves and depended less on their landlords' advice. When problems did arise, they were apt to consult the village agricultural advisor instead, a trained specialist hired jointly by the village office and the local agricultural association to promote and coordinate farming improvements.[84] Local police and officials from the village office were available to settle disputes. Increasingly, government

81. *Okayama ken kosaku kankō*, pp. 85-86, 88.
82. Interview with Kubo Yasuo.
83. Wagatsuma Tosaku, "Jinushi seido to buraku seido no kankei," *Teikoku nōkai hō* 33 (May 1943): 8.
84. Embree, *Suye Mura*, p. 63.

agencies took over responsibility for crop insurance and disaster relief.[85]

Thus, even if not absentee in a physical sense, many landlords became absentee owners in a functional sense, no longer as important as they once had been as community leaders and protectors of their tenants. As the interests and activities of landlords and tenants diverged, harmony and cooperation between them began to break down. Only when both parties made a special effort to maintain personal contact, or in remote villages relatively untouched by change, did traditional ties remain fully in force.

85. Amano Fujio, *Nōson shakai mondai: jinushi to kosakunin* (Tokyo, 1920), p. 10; Tōbata, *Nōchi o meguru,* pp. 70-72; by the same author, *Nihon shihonshugi no keisei sha,* pp. 136-37.

CHAPTER FIVE

Landlord-Tenant Conflict

The Regional Character of Landlord-Tenant Conflict

Tenancy disputes, which had occurred sporadically in the past few decades, began to increase in number in the mid-Taishō era. Only 85 disputes had been reported in 1917. In 1926 the figure had climbed to 2,751, and in 1935, to 6,824. In all, some 72,000 disputes were reported between 1917 and 1941.[1] Some of these disputes involved little more than the presentation of petitions; others, rarely more than 100 or so a year, were long, drawn-out affairs, involving violent confrontations between landlords and tenants. The vast majority of disputes fell between these two extremes.

To keep abreast of unrest in the countryside after World War I, the Japanese government required annual information from prefectural officials on the number and nature of disputes within their jurisdictions. Observers were dispatched fairly regularly from Tokyo to make on-the-spot assessments of disputes in progress; their reports, classified as secret at the time but released during the Occupation, contain frank discussion of the issues and individuals

1. Nōmin undō shi kenkyū kai, *Nihon nōmin undō shi,* p. 120 (Table 1), based on data in Nōrinshō, nōmukyoku, *Kosaku nenpō, 1932* (Tokyo, 1933) and *Nōchi nenpō, 1941* (Tokyo, 1942). The above figure includes Hokkaido, where 3,173 disputes occurred between 1917 and 1941, and Okinawa, where only 2 disputes (both in 1939) occurred. Tables 11-17 in this chapter include Hokkaido; Tables 13-17 include Okinawa as well.

involved. These government materials—and other materials compiled less systematically by scholars, journalists and officers of the
Imperial Agricultural Association—provide a fairly comprehensive
record. Although not without flaws and ambiguities, the record
permits relatively detailed analysis of the nature of landlord-tenant
conflict. It reveals, first of all, that there were pronounced regional
differences in both the incidence and nature of tenancy disputes.

Between 1917 and 1931 disputes were concentrated in central
Honshu. Close to 60 percent of the total number occurred in the
Kinki and Chubu regions;[2] only 8 percent occurred in the Tohoku,
with even fewer disputes reported from other outlying regions of the
country (Table 11). There were no disputes in the Tohoku in 1917;
between 1918 and 1926, only 134. In contrast, there were 5,097
disputes in the Kinki between 1917 and 1926, 40 percent of the
total number in the nation in those years.[3]

There were almost twice as many disputes between 1932 and 1941
as there had been between 1917 and 1931. By far the greatest
increase occurred in the Tohoku, which now ranked first in the
nation with over 12,000 disputes. Other outlying regions of the
country, too, experienced more unrest than in the previous decade.
In contrast, the number of disputes in the Kinki declined by 26
percent. In the Chubu region, disputes increased in number, but at
a rate markedly below that occurring elsewhere (Table 12).[4]

Paralleling this shift in the incidence of disputes was a marked
change in their nature. Roughly half of all disputes between 1917
and 1931 were triggered by poor harvests (Table 13). In most disputes (over 70 percent of the total between 1923 and 1931) tenants

2. The Chubu consists of Niigata, Toyama, Ishikawa, Fukui, Nagano, Yamanashi,
Shizuoka, Gifu and Aichi Prefectures.
3. Teikoku nōkai, "Kosaku sōgi jinushi kosakunin kumiai kosaku chōtei ni
kansuru shiryō," *Teikoku nōkai hō* 27 (June 1937): 360–62.
4. A shift occurred in the location of disputes within the Chubu. Between 1917 and
1931 over 43 percent of disputes in the region were in Gifu and Aichi Prefectures;
between 1932 and 1941, however, these two prefectures accounted for only 17 percent of disputes. Yamanashi and Nagano Prefectures, where 20 percent of disputes
occurred between 1917 and 1931, now accounted for over 48 percent. Calculated
from data in *Kosaku nenpō, 1932* and *Nōchi nenpō, 1941*.

TABLE 11.

Regional Distribution of Tenancy Disputes,
1917–1931

Rank	Region	Number of disputes	Percentage of total
1	Kinki	8,729	34.9
2	Chubu	5,765	23.1
3	Kanto	2,586	10.3
4	Chugoku	2,011	8.0
5	Tohoku	2,001	8.0
6	Kyushu	1,987	8.0
7	Shikoku	1,416	5.7
8	Hokkaido	493	2.0
	Total	24,988	100.0

Source: Nōrinshō, nōmukyoku, *Kosaku nenpō,*
1931 and *1934.*

demanded temporary or permanent rent reductions (Table 14). Furthermore, these disputes were large in scale, each one involving on the average some fifty tenants, thirteen landlords, and thirty-four *chō* of land (Tables 15 and 16).[5] Typically, tenants were organized into unions. Instead of seeking individual agreements with their landlords, they now insisted on collective bargaining.[6]

Between 1932 and 1941, however, the number of disputes triggered by poor harvests decreased, accounting for only 24 percent of all disputes. In contrast, the number of disputes triggered by attempted evictions increased more than fivefold, accounting for

5. If one examines prefectural, not nationwide, data, it is clear that substantial percentages of tenant farmers (both landless tenants and owner-tenants) were involved in disputes in some portions of the country. In 1926, for example, only 4 percent of all tenants in the nation participated in disputes. But in Osaka 32 percent of tenants were involved; in Nara, 23 percent; Kyoto, 19 percent; and Hyogo, 13 percent. *Kosaku nenpō, 1926* (Table 15).

6. Ogura Takekazu, *Tochi rippō no shiteki kōsatsu* (Tokyo, 1951), p. 359. For data on tenant unions see Nōchi kaikaku kiroku iinkai, ed., *Nōchi kaikaku tenmatsu gaiyō* (Tokyo, 1951), p. 62.

TABLE 12.
Regional Distribution of Tenancy Disputes,
1932–1941

Rank	Region	Number of disputes	Percentage of total	Index (no. of disputes 1917–1931 as 100)
1	Tohoku	12,320	25.8	616
2	Chubu	8,682	18.2	151
3	Kinki	6,491	13.6	74
4	Kanto	6,127	12.8	237
5	Kyushu	4,620	9.7	233
6	Chugoku	3,554	7.5	177
7	Shikoku	3,230	6.8	228
8	Hokkaido	2,680	5.6	544
	Total	47,704	100.0	

Source: Nōrinshō, nōmukyoku, *Kosaku nenpō, 1934* and *Nōchi nenpō, 1941.* The above total does not include two disputes which occurred in Okinawa in 1939.

slightly more than 50 percent of the total (Table 13).[7] Reflecting this change, the principal demand of tenant farmers shifted from rent reduction to the continuation of tenancy or to compensation when tenancy was terminated (Table 14). Although disputes increased in number, they declined markedly in scale: each dispute involved on the average only thirteen tenants, four landlords, and nine *chō* of land (Tables 15 and 16). Union activity slackened as well. Indeed, membership in tenant unions had begun to decline in 1928.[8]

What these data on the nature of disputes indicate is the existence of two distinct types of landlord-tenant conflict: 1) large-scale disputes over rents, which prevailed between 1917 and 1931, and 2)

7. Or almost 62 percent, if one includes disputes triggered by rent arrears (in which landlords usually threatened tenants with eviction).
8. *Nōchi kaikaku tenmatsu gaiyō,* p. 62. Membership in tenant unions reached a peak of 365,332 in 1927; in 1935, membership was 242,422; in 1941, 23,595. Government arrests of tenant union leaders in the late 1920s were certainly a factor in the decline of the union movement.

97

TABLE 13.
Immediate Causes of Disputes,
1920–1941

Causes of disputes	1920–1931		1932–1941	
	Number	% of Total	Number	% of Total
1 Crop failure or poor harvest	12,389	50.9	11,286	23.7
2 Attempted eviction of tenants	4,433	18.2	23,994	50.3
3 High rents or lack of uniformity in local rent levels	2,045	8.4	1,253	2.6
4 Current trends of thought[a]	1,109	4.6	103	0.2
5 Decline in farm prices	951	3.9	118	0.3
6 Rent arrears	600	2.5	5,401	11.3
7 Rent increases	565	2.3	1,397	2.9
8 Inadequate compensation for tenant farming	528	2.2	380	0.8
9 Rice inspection	214	0.9	337	0.7
10 Land (paddy) adjustment	123	0.5	105	0.2
11 Other	1,364	5.6	3,332	7.0
Total reported	24,321	100.0	47,706	100.0

Source: See Nōmin undō shi kenkyū kai, ed., *Nihon nōmin undō shi* (Tokyo, 1961), p. 15 (Table 2), for a tabulation of reported causes of disputes compiled from data published in annual editions of *Kosaku nenpō*. In the original data only one cause for each dispute was cited, and how that was determined is unclear. Since case studies of disputes, including those published by the government, generally cite several major causes for each dispute, one cannot regard the above data as conclusive. It is probably not inaccurate to assume that only the most immediate cause of each dispute was cited.

[a]"Current trends of thought" (*moyō*) refers to changes in the attitudes of tenant farmers: the development of class consciousness, increased emphasis on rights as opposed to obligations, and the organization of tenant unions demanding collective bargaining with landlords. See Teikoku nōkai chōsa bu, "Kosaku sōgi ni kansuru chōsa," *Teikoku nōkai hō* 12 (June 1922): 42.

TABLE 14.
Principal Demands of Tenants, 1923–1941

Year	Total number of disputes	Temporary rent reductions		Permanent rent reductions		Continuation of tenancy or compensation	
		Number	%	Number	%	Number	%
1923	1,917	1,249	65.2	582	30.4	15	0.8
1924	1,532	1,044	68.1	358	23.4	35	2.3
1925	2,206	1,444	65.4	475	21.5	173	7.8
1926	2,751	2,011	73.1	272	9.9	318	11.6
1927	2,052	1,206	58.8	253	12.3	444	21.6
1928	1,866	1,014	54.3	177	9.5	484	25.9
1929	2,434	1,339	55.0	151	6.2	728	29.9
1930	2,478	1,042	42.0	192	7.7	1,030	41.6
1931	3,419	1,609	47.0	166	4.9	1,363	39.9
1932	3,414	1,267	37.1	121	3.5	1,468	43.0
1933	4,000	1,013	25.3	127	3.2	2,305	57.6
1934	5,828	2,168	37.2	109	1.9	2,668	45.8
1935	6,824	2,616	38.3	105	1.5	3,055	44.8
1936	6,804	1,621	23.8	213	3.1	3,674	54.0
1937	6,170	1,318	21.4	230	3.7	3,509	56.9
1938	4,615	1,064	23.0	157	3.4	2,421	52.5
1939	3,578	711	19.9	230	6.4	1,645	46.0
1940	3,165	767	24.2	243	7.8	1,412	44.6
1941	3,308	867	26.2	294	8.9	1,316	39.8

Source: Nōrinshō, nōmukyoku, *Kosaku nenpō*, 1932 and *Nōchi nenpō*, 1941, tabulated in Nōmin undō shi kenkyū kai, ed., *Nihon nōmin undō shi*, p. 121 (Table 2).

small-scale disputes over arable land itself, which prevailed between 1932 and 1941. Moreover, just as disputes as a whole were unevenly distributed throughout the country, so too were these different kinds of landlord-tenant conflict. Disputes over rents were especially numerous in the Kinki and Chubu regions. In 1926, for example, over 80 percent of all disputes in the Kinki were triggered by poor harvests and involved tenant demands for rent reductions.[9] In contrast,

9. *Kosaku nenpō, 1926* (Table 2).

TABLE 15.
Participants in Tenancy Disputes, 1920–1941

Year	Number of disputes	Landlords		Tenants	
		Total number	Number per dispute	Total number	Number per dispute
1920	408	5,236	12.8	34,605	84.8
1921	1,680	33,985	20.2	145,898	86.8
1922	1,578	29,077	18.4	125,750	79.7
1923	1,917	31,712	16.5	134,503	70.2
1924	1,532	27,223	17.8	110,920	72.4
1925	2,206	33,001	15.0	134,646	61.0
1926	2,751	39,705	14.4	151,061	54.9
1927	2,052	24,136	11.8	91,336	44.5
1928	1,866	19,474	10.4	75,136	40.3
1929	2,434	23,505	9.7	81,998	33.7
1930	2,478	14,159	5.7	58,565	23.6
1931	3,419	23,768	6.9	81,135	23.7
sub-total	24,321	304,981	12.5	1,225,553	50.4
1932	3,414	16,706	4.9	61,499	18.0
1933	4,000	14,312	3.6	48,073	12.0
1934	5,828	34,035	5.8	121,031	20.8
1935	6,824	28,574	4.2	113,164	16.6
1936	6,804	23,293	3.4	77,187	11.3
1937	6,170	20,230	3.3	63,246	10.3
1938	4,615	15,422	3.3	52,817	11.4
1939	3,578	9,065	2.5	25,904	7.2
1940	3,165	11,082	3.5	38,614	12.2
1941	3,308	11,037	3.3	32,289	9.8
sub-total	47,706	183,756	3.9	633,824	13.3

Source: Nōrinshō, nōmukyoku, *Kosaku nenpō*, 1932 and *Nōchi nenpō*, 1941, tabulated in Nōmin undō shi kenkyū kai, ed. *Nihon nōmin undō shi*, p. 123 (Table 3).

TABLE 16.
Area of Land Involved in Disputes, 1920–1941
(in chō*)*

Year	Number of disputes	Total area	Area per dispute
1920	408	27,390	67.1
1921	1,680	88,681	52.8
1922	1,578	90,253	57.2
1923	1,917	89,080	46.5
1924	1,532	70,387	45.9
1925	2,206	95,941	43.5
1926	2,751	95,653	34.8
1927	2,052	59,169	28.8
1928	1,866	48,694	26.1
1929	2,434	56,831	23.4
1930	2,478	39,799	16.1
1931	3,419	60,365	17.7
subtotal	24,321	822,243	33.8
1932	3,414	39,028	11.4
1933	4,000	30,596	7.7
1934	5,828	85,838	14.7
1935	6,824	70,745	10.4
1936	6,804	46,420	6.8
1937	6,170	39,582	6.4
1938	4,615	34,359	7.4
1939	3,578	16,623	4.6
1940	3,165	27,625	8.7
1941	3,308	21,898	6.6
subtotal	47,706	412,714	8.7

Source: Nōrinshō, nōmukyoku, *Kosaku nenpō,*
1931 and *Nōchi nenpō,* 1941, tabulated in Nōmin
undō shi kenkyū kai, ed., *Nihon nōmin undō shi,*
p. 125 (Table 4). The above figures for area include
all types of agricultural land.

eviction disputes predominated in the Tohoku, in some years accounting for over 70 percent of all disputes reported in the region.[10]
Unlike central Honshu, where disputes in both the 1920s and 1930s
were large in scale, disputes in the Tohoku were extremely small
in scale, involving only one or two tenants, a single landlord, and
very little land.[11] Finally, although tenant unions were formed in the
Tohoku, they never rivaled those of the Kinki or Chubu regions in
number or membership.[12] In my view, it is no coincidence that these
regional differences in landlord-tenant conflict correspond to regional differences among landlords themselves.

Landlord-Tenant Conflict, 1917–1931

It is generally agreed that tenants took the initiative in launching
disputes during the 1920s. Their new assertiveness, while not a
harbinger of revolution as some writers have maintained,[13] clearly
revealed an important change in authority relations in the Japanese
countryside. Tenants no longer accepted their subordinate status
meekly. Rather, they now confronted landlords en masse, demanding that their grievances be heard.

As I have argued elsewhere,[14] this assertiveness among tenants
was not the product of desperate poverty. On the contrary, disputes

10. In 1934, 70 percent of all disputes in the Tohoku involved evictions, compared
to only 16 percent in the Kinki; in 1937, 78 percent of disputes in the Tohoku and
22 percent in the Kinki involved evictions. *Nihon nōmin undō shi,* p. 52 (Table 4).

11. In Aomori Prefecture in 1935, for example, each dispute involved an average
of .95 landlords, 1.6 tenants and 1.09 *chō* of land. In Hyogo Prefecture in the same
year an average of 10.6 landlords, 29.6 tenants and 13.6 *chō* of land were involved
in each dispute. Calculated from data in *Kosaku nenpō, 1935,* Appendix 2, pp. 4–5
(Table 2).

12. In 1935, there were 502 tenant unions in the Kinki, with a membership of
27,645. In contrast, there were only 388 unions in the Tohoku, with 18,264 members.
Yet in that year over 1,500 disputes were reported in the Tohoku, more than twice
the number in the Kinki. *Nōchi nenpō,* 1940, pp. 68–71; Appendix 2, pp. 2–3.

13. I think many Japanese writers have focused undue attention on the relatively
few violent disputes that occurred, especially those in which labor union leaders
and left-wing intellectuals took part.

14. Ann Waswo, "Origins of Tenant Unrest," in *Japan in Crisis: Essays on
Taishō Democracy,* eds. B. Silberman and H. Harootunian (Princeton, 1974),
pp. 374–79.

in the 1920s generally were more numerous where the economic conditions of tenancy, and of farming itself, were relatively good. Similarly, the behavior of tenants cannot be attributed to the long-term effects of such Meiji reforms as universal education alone. The six years of schooling required of all Japanese no doubt had an impact on tenant farmers, making them less dependent on their social superiors for assistance in daily life and causing those among them who had excelled in the classroom to resent the status and power of their "betters." But these effects, like the educational system itself, were nationwide in scope. Yet disputes were concentrated in the Kinki and Chubu. To understand why tenants launched disputes, therefore, one should consider the specific conditions prevailing in these two regions.

In the Kinki and Chubu were four of the seven most highly industrialized prefectures in the country in the early twentieth century.[15] Here, too, the new trends among landlords discussed in the previous chapter—their abandonment of farming, involvement in non-agricultural affairs, and increased absentee ownership— were most pronounced. Both the development of industry and the dissociation of landlords from rural life had an important bearing on the outbreak of disputes.

Industrial development in and around such major cities as Osaka, Kobe and Nagoya—in particular, the rapid expansion of industry during World War I—affected local tenant farmers in several ways. Most basically, increased job opportunities in factories attracted tenants, or their children, to the cities, reducing the competition for land among those who remained behind in the villages. The latter could then demand lower rents or other improvements in tenancy conditions with little fear of reprisals: their landlords, unable to find tenants to replace them, would be constrained to agree to their demands.[16]

The increase in urban job opportunities also reduced the tenants' economic dependence on farming. Believing that they could find

15. The four were Aichi, Kyoto, Osaka and Hyogo.
16. Tōbata Seiichi, *Nōchi o meguru jinushi to nōmin* (Tokyo, 1947), p. 66.

103

work in factories, they were less reluctant than they had been in the past to confront their landlords with demands. Near Osaka, for example, improvements in local transportation made it easier for tenants to travel to the city for work, and increases in factory wages after 1914 gave them an incentive to do so. Armed with the security of alternative employment, they initiated a number of disputes.[17] In a village in Aichi Prefecture in 1922, tenants formed a labor gang and threatened to embark for Nagoya if landlords did not reduce rents.[18]

Moreover, the experience of working as wage laborers affected tenants' attitudes toward farming in ways that contributed to landlord-tenant conflict. In Hyogo Prefecture, for example, many tenants left their villages during World War I to work as unskilled laborers in the rapidly expanding shipping industry in Kobe, leaving farming to the women and old men in their families. They found that it was possible to earn a good livelihood from wage labor, and in 1919 they began to demand that landlords reduce rents so that farming, too, could become profitable.[19] In a village in Fukui Prefecture where a dispute occurred in 1920, local police reported that many tenants had been working part-time in nearby textile mills and, as a result, had become more "cunning" than ordinary tenants and less content with the existing tenancy system.[20] As officials in Aichi Prefecture observed:

The basic cause of most disputes is the awareness among tenants that agricultural labor is much more troublesome than other kinds of labor and that farming itself is much less profitable than other occupations. Poor harvests merely provide tenants with an immediate excuse for pressing their grievances.[21]

17. Nōshōmushō, nōmukyoku, *Kosaku sōgi ni kansuru chōsa* 2 (Tokyo, 1922): 18. Hereafter abbreviated KS.

18. Aichi ken nōchi hensen iinkai, *Aichi ken nōchi shi* 1 (Nagoya, 1957): 452–53.

19. KS 2: 51.

20. KS 1: 234. Tenants also learned such new techniques of protest as the preparation of itemized lists of grievances and detailed accounts of their income and expenses from their experience as factory workers. See KS 2: 60–61.

21. KS 2: 128.

The end of the wartime boom in the early 1920s introduced new elements of unrest. As factories curtailed production and unskilled workers lost their jobs, tenant farmers who had come to depend on wage earnings to maintain a higher standard of living found it necessary to retrench. Agricultural prices, which had risen during the war, now declined, and tenants who raised secondary crops for commercial sale found themselves with reduced incomes. Unable to protest effectively against general economic conditions, these tenants turned instead to the most immediate problem they faced, the rents they paid their landlords, and demanded rent reductions.[22]

But tenants were not moved to launch disputes solely by prevailing economic conditions or by their discovery that farming was troublesome and unprofitable. The available data suggest that underlying these more rational complaints were grievances of an emotional nature, directed against landlords themselves and against the impersonal nature of landlord-tenant relations.

Sugiyama Motojirō, founder and head of the Japan Farmers' Union, observed in 1926 that more disputes occurred on land owned by absentee landlords than on land owned by village residents.[23] Although no comprehensive survey of the kinds of landlords involved in disputes was ever undertaken, frequent references to the problem of absentee ownership in the case studies of disputes published by the Ministry of Agriculture tend to substantiate his claim.

In a few of these case studies inferior tenancy conditions on absentee-owned land are cited as the cause of disputes.[24] Moreover, it is possible that some tenants engaged in disputes with absentee landlords for tactical reasons. Having other sources of income and lacking the interest or ability to farm their own land, absentee landlords generally were more willing to grant tenant demands for rent

22. KS 2: 59; *Nihon nōmin undō shi,* pp. 33–34, 516.
23. "Mazu fuzai jinushi o naku seyo," *Nōsei kenkyū* 5 (1926): 23. See also Kyōchōkai, nōsonka, *Kosaku mondai o chūshin ni mitaru nōmin shisō* (Tokyo, 1933), p. 4, where the authors note that one basic cause of disputes was the landlords' abandonment both of farming and of the lifestyle of farmers.
24. For examples see KS 1: 123, 398.

reductions than resident landlords. Once a settlement favorable to the tenants had been reached, the tenants could demand similar terms from resident landlords, arguing persuasively that rent levels should be the same on equivalent grades of land, regardless of ownership.[25]

But the most common reason cited for these disputes was the hostility of tenant farmers toward absentee landlords who showed little interest in local affairs. As discussed previously, the tenants of absentee landlords usually paid no more in rent than tenants of resident landlords while enjoying greater security of tenure. But apparently these economic advantages were not as meaningful to them as personal relations with their landlords, precisely what absentee landlords could not provide.

Observers in southern Okayama Prefecture noted the absence of "feelings of friendship and intimacy" between absentee landlords and their tenants as a cause of disputes.[26] That over 60 percent of all landlords in a village in Yamanashi Prefecture were absentee owners who did not display traditional paternalism was regarded as the basic cause of disputes.[27] Similarly, the existence of many absentee landlords who failed to provide leadership and financial aid in their village was one cause of a dispute in Aichi Prefecture in 1917.[28]

Landlords who remained in the village but no longer performed customary functions also experienced more disputes than traditional village landlords. In some cases tenant resentment was intensified because these landlords still claimed the prerogatives which their functions had justified in the past. A report from Hyogo Prefecture, for example, portrayed most local landlords as "bigots" because they sat in chairs when their tenants came to see them but made the tenants sit on the floor.[29] In Gifu Prefecture landlords "treated

25. Ibid., p. 424; Okayama ken naimubu, *Okayama ken kosaku kankō chōsa sho* (Okayama, 1924), p. 92.
26. KS 1: 314.
27. Ibid., p. 192.
28. Ibid., p. 95.
29. KS 2: 65.

tenants in the manner of feudal lords dealing with their retainers," some of them not even letting tenants enter the room they occupied. But this type of behavior, now considered haughty by tenants, had been considered entirely appropriate only a short time earlier. Indeed, Gifu tenants had formerly called landlords *tsuchi oya,* or fathers of the land, and treated them with all the deference due a feudal lord. The crucial difference now was that landlords appeared uninterested in their tenants' affairs and did little or nothing to command their respect.[30]

In other cases, however, it was not the haughtiness of resident landlords that aroused tenant resentment, but the very absence of landlord-tenant contact. Landlords in a village in Yamanashi Prefecture were "too intent on making money" to see their tenants.[31] All the landlords involved in a dispute in 1920 in Fukui Prefecture were residents of their village, but they were considered "absentee owners" by their tenants because they lived on the shopping street of the village, ran small businesses, and displayed no interest in farming.[32]

Responses to Tenant Militancy in the 1920s

The available data indicate that landlords did not win very many tenancy disputes in the 1920s (Table 17). Between 1920 and 1931 24,321 disputes were reported. In only 406, less than 2 percent of the total, did landlords emerge victorious. The great majority of

---

30. Ibid., pp. 173–76. Similarly, observers noted that most resident landlords in a village in Aichi Prefecture studied the tea ceremony, not agriculture; only two or three of them helped their tenants build compost sheds. KS 1: 94–95.

31. KS 2: 200.

32. KS 1: 230–34. Yet another source of tenant resentment is suggested by a report on a dispute in Awajika village, Hyogo Prefecture. There, most tenants were cultivating land which they had once owned themselves but which they had lost to a local landlord by defaulting on loans. These tenants, according to the report, had long been looking for an opportunity to "get even" with the landlord for what had happened. They found such an opportunity when rice inspection was instituted in 1917. The observers concluded, however, that the basic cause of the dispute that ensued was the already strained relationship between the landlord and his tenants. KS 1: 26–39. Detailed case studies of tenancy disputes and of the kinds of tenants taking part in them are needed, I think, to improve our understanding of the causes and nature of tenant unrest.

TABLE 17.
The Results of Tenancy Disputes,
1920–1941

Year	Number of disputes	Compromise		Tenant victory		Tenant defeat		Not settled	
		No.	%	No.	%	No.	%	No.	%
1920	408	255	62.5	53	13.0	5	1.2	79	19.4
1921	1,680	1,340	79.8	109	6.5	14	0.8	191	11.4
1922	1,578	815	51.6	86	5.4	—	—	593	37.6
1923	1,917	1,451	75.7	89	4.6	32	1.7	319	16.6
1924	1,532	1,148	74.9	75	4.9	32	2.0	253	16.5
1925	2,206	1,625	73.7	93	4.2	13	0.6	436	19.8
1926	2,751	2,025	73.6	101	3.7	20	0.7	582	21.2
1927	2,052	1,371	66.8	56	2.7	9	0.4	593	28.9
1928	1,866	1,261	67.6	60	3.2	29	1.6	513	27.5
1929	2,434	1,615	66.4	127	5.2	63	2.6	614	25.2
1930	2,478	1,235	49.8	410	16.5	106	4.3	702	28.3
1931	3,419	2,078	60.8	417	12.2	83	2.4	815	23.8
1932	3,414	2,101	61.5	481	14.1	61	1.8	718	21.0
1933	4,000	2,568	64.2	523	13.1	92	2.3	761	19.0
1934	5,828	3,764	64.6	922	15.8	157	2.7	909	15.6
1935	6,824	5,131	75.2	381	5.6	160	2.3	1,070	15.7
1936	6,804	5,162	75.9	294	4.3	167	2.4	1,109	16.3
1937	6,170	4,824	78.2	277	4.5	107	1.7	886	14.4
1938	4,615	3,619	78.4	264	5.7	86	1.9	595	12.9
1939	3,578	2,960	82.7	136	3.8	93	2.6	337	9.4
1940	3,165	2,120	67.0	469	14.8	86	2.7	442	14.0
1941	3,308	2,232	67.5	659	19.9	182	5.5	82	2.5

Sources: Nishida Yoshiaki, "Nōchi kaikaku no rekishiteki seikaku," in Rekishigaku kenkyū kai, *Rekishi ni okeru minzoku to minshushugi* (November 1973), p. 161; Saitō Isamu, "Nihon nōmin undō no jiki kubun ni tsuite no shiron," *Keizai kagaku* (1958), p. 34, based on data in Nōrinshō, nōmukyoku, *Kosaku nenpō* and *Nōchi nenpō,* 1920–1941. Not included among the results given above are two minor categories: "natural extinction" (*shizen shōmetsu*) and "return of land" (cited infrequently in the 1920s and equivalent in most, but not all, cases to tenant defeat). Therefore, the results given for any one year do not add up to the total number of disputes for that year, nor do the percentages given total 100 percent.

disputes, 70 percent of the total, ended in compromise. It was generally recognized at the time, however, that compromise settlements represented victories for tenants, not landlords.[33] This was certainly the case in disputes involving tenant demands for rent reductions—that is, in over 70 percent of all disputes in the 1920s. Tenants might demand, for example, a rent reduction of 30 percent and settle, by means of compromise, for a reduction of 20 percent. At any rate, they emerged from the dispute paying less rent than before, and landlords emerged with less income. What these figures on the results of disputes indicate is that tenants—despite the absence of legal recognition of their right to form unions and engage in collective bargaining, indeed despite the absence of legal protection per se—nonetheless enjoyed certain advantages in conflict with landlords.

The very novelty of disputes, especially in the early 1920s, appears to have worked to the advantage of tenants. Landlords, who were accustomed to deference from their tenants and to individual bargaining, lacked a strategy for dealing with demands presented by organized groups. As they groped to understand what was happening and to determine how they should react, tenants were able to maintain the initiative.

The timing of disputes gave tenants a further edge. Most disputes in the 1920s erupted in the autumn, after crops were harvested but before rents were due. In 1921, for example, 1,421 of 1,680 disputes occurred between October and December.[34] Tenants entered disputes, then, with their own basic food supply on hand. Unlike industrial workers who could not survive for long without wages (or a strike fund), tenants were in a position to hold out for acceptance of their demands. By comparison, their landlords, especially smaller landlords who possessed little or no reserves of food or money at year's end, were under considerable pressure to reach a settlement.[35]

---

33. *Kosaku nenpō, 1931,* p. 27.
34. *Nihon nōmin undō shi,* p. 254.
35. Hayashi Chūtarō, "Kosaku mondai ni kansuru kōsatsu," *Teikoku nōkai hō* 11 (November 1921): 28.

The large scale of tenancy disputes in this decade, not infrequently involving most of the tenants and tenanted land in a community, provided tenants with additional leverage. Having agreed on a united front among themselves, tenants could threaten to abandon cultivation of their fields the following year if their demands were not met, knowing that landlords would be hard put to find new tenants to replace them. Unless landlords had other sources of income or were in a position to farm their own holdings, they would once again be constrained to settle the dispute quickly. Moreover, it was usually possible for tenants to persuade at least a few landlords from among those whose land was involved in the dispute—for example, an absentee owner with no interest in farming or a local shopkeeper who feared a tenant boycott of his business—to agree to their demands fairly rapidly. Then tenants could exert pressure on the remaining landlords to follow suit.[36] Indeed, it appears to have been a conscious strategy among tenants to exploit differences among landlords as a means of overcoming resistance to their demands.

In time, of course, landlords developed an arsenal of countermeasures to offset the advantages tenants enjoyed in disputes. Chief among these was the formation of landlord unions (*jinushi kumiai*), their own united front. Joint action among landlords was by no means a new development. Landlords had banded together in the early Meiji period to study farming improvements, and a large number of landlord associations had been formed in the first decade of the twentieth century to establish rice inspection. In their stated objectives the landlord unions formed in the 1920s differed little from these earlier organizations. They, too, proclaimed an interest in improving tenancy conditions, promoting agriculture, and fostering good will and harmony among all members of rural society.[37] Nonetheless, there were important differences.

In the Meiji era large landlords had taken the initiative in

36. Arimoto Hideo, "Kosakunō no zokusuru jinushi sū ni tsuite," *Teikoku nōkai hō* 11 (October 1921): 13–14.
37. *Nōchi kaikaku tenmatsu gaiyō*, pp. 67–68.

organizing landlord associations. Now, however, small landlords, who were in the weakest position when disputes arose, became the principal advocates of landlord cooperation.[38] Associations which had once been open to all landowners, whether landlords or owner-cultivators, now were restricted to the owners of leased land.[39] The activities of earlier associations, while clearly promoting the interests of their members, often benefited tenant farmers and the community as a whole—by achieving increased productivity, for example, or by obtaining new markets for local crops. Despite their stated objectives, however, the landlord unions formed in the 1920s did little to promote agriculture or to improve tenancy conditions. Their efforts to foster good will and harmony among all members of rural society did not include recognition of the validity of tenant grievances. Rather, most landlord unions of the 1920s placed full blame for rural unrest on the tenants themselves, or on outside agitators; their purpose was to destroy the organized tenant movement.[40]

This purpose is clearly revealed by the activities of landlord unions. According to a government survey conducted in 1926, the bylaws of most landlord unions contained the following provisions: 1) when tenants made "unjust" demands, landlords would demand the return of their land; 2) returned land would be cultivated jointly by all landlords in the union; 3) no union member would be allowed to act independently in granting rent reductions, deferring rent payments, or ordering evictions; 4) all members would contribute to a defense fund to be used when disputes arose; and 5) any member violating the bylaws would be fined.[41]

In addition, the bylaws of some landlord unions contained provisions for filing suit against tenants who refused to pay their rents and for the automatic eviction of tenant union leaders. If tenants

38. Nōrinshō, nōmukyoku, *Jinushi kosakunin kumiai undō no gaiyō* (Tokyo, 1928), pp. 2-3.

39. See Nōrinshō, nōmukyoku, *Jinushi kosakunin kumiai kiyaku jirei* (Tokyo, 1926), pp. 103-25, for examples of this and other restrictions.

40. *Nōchi kaikaku tenmatsu gaiyō*, p. 68; Nōshōmushō, nōmukyoku, *Jinushi kumiai ni kansuru chōsa* (Tokyo, 1921), p. 47.

41. *Jinushi kosakunin kumiai kiyaku jirei*, pp. 98-99.

111

threatened to abandon cultivation of one landlord's fields, all the landlords who leased land to those tenants would demand that their fields be returned as well. If land returned to landlords could not be cultivated, either by means of hired labor or cooperative effort among the landlords, all taxes due on that land would be paid by the union.[42]

Another step taken by landlords was the formation of land companies (*tochi gaisha*). The avowed purpose of these companies was "to plan for conciliation and harmony between landlords and tenants, thereby promoting the prosperity of both."[43] But actually they were designed to strengthen the landlords' position in tenancy disputes. Landlords in a given locality, typically a village or hamlet, turned over the management of their holdings to a company which then leased the land to tenants and collected rents. Unlike landlord unions, which as voluntary associations had no legal rights, land companies were organized as partnerships or as joint stock companies. As such, they were recognized as legal entities under the civil and commercial codes and could engage more effectively in litigation.[44] To challenge a land company tenants had to be prepared for a long and costly legal battle which they were likely to lose in the end. Nor was it as easy for them to exploit personal differences among landlords since the latter were now represented by a single bargaining agent.

Not surprisingly, the majority of landlord unions and land companies organized in the 1920s were to be found in those regions of the country where tenancy disputes were the most numerous. In 1928, for example, there were 160 landlord unions in the Kinki district, where tenant unrest was severe; only 32 existed in the Tohoku, as yet relatively untouched by disputes.[45] From both their regional concentration and their activities, it is clear that landlord

42. Ibid., p. 99.
43. *Jinushi kosakunin kumiai undō no gaiyō,* p. 38.
44. Ibid.; see also *Nōchi kaikaku tenmatsu gaiyō,* pp. 68–69, and Kyōchōkai, nōsonka, *Honpō saikin no shakai undō* (Tokyo, 1930), p. 407.
45. *Jinushi kosakunin kumiai undō no gaiyō,* p. 82 (Table 1). Like landlord unions, land companies were also most numerous in southwestern Japan. Of the 85 companies in existence in 1929, 45 were located in the Kinki; only 5 were located

unions and land companies were combative responses to tenant unrest.

By the mid-1920s landlords had also devised a variety of what may be termed preemptive measures to deal with tenant unrest. Particularly in regions where few disputes had yet occurred, landlords were active in organizing conciliation associations (*kyōchō kumiai*) in which both landlords and tenants participated. In 1926 there were 1,491 of these associations with a total membership (including both landlords and tenants) of 164,585.[46] In some cases an association consisted of only one landlord, usually a large-scale landowner, and all his tenants. But the majority contained several small landlords and the tenants who leased parcels of land from each of them. In their operation these associations provided a mechanism for the peaceful resolution of differences between landlords and tenants. Potentially divisive issues—rent levels, the rate of rent reductions when crops were poor, the terms of tenancy contracts—which might otherwise trigger disputes were decided by discussion.[47] Unlike landlords who organized unions, then, landlords who organized conciliation associations were prepared to some degree to admit the validity of tenant grievances. Rather than attacking tenants, they were prepared to work with them. Nevertheless, an element of cooptation was also involved: in many cases, landlords formed conciliation associations to forestall the organization of tenant unions.[48] By involving tenants in a joint enterprise over which they expected to exert considerable influence, these landlords hoped to prevent the creation of a united front among tenants against themselves.

A second preemptive measure, employed by landlords on an individual basis, was the sale of small parcels of land to tenants. In Okayama Prefecture, for example, a number of landlords started

---

in the Tohoku. Nōrinshō, nōmukyoku, *Nōchi kankei tochi gaisha oyobi ukeoi kosaku ni kansuru chōsa* (Tokyo, 1932), pp. 151–54 (Table 4).

46. *Nōchi kaikaku tenmatsu gaiyō*, p. 70.

47. Ibid., pp. 69–71; see also *Jinushi kosakunin kumiai undō no gaiyō*, pp. 43–46.

48. Sunaga Shigemitsu, ed., *Kindai Nihon no jinushi to nōmin* (Tokyo, 1966), p. 371; Yamagata ken keizaibu, *Kosaku jijō to nōmin undō* (Yamagata, 1940), p. 60.

savings funds for their tenants in the 1920s, depositing each year the proceeds from the sale of a portion of the rent rice tenants paid so that tenants would eventually be able to purchase land.[49] Although the ostensible reason for these arrangements was to promote the creation of owner-cultivators, the amount of money involved was usually so small that tenants could expect at best to acquire only a *tan* or two of land after many years; they would still need to lease additional land to make a living. One may infer then that landlords hoped by means of these arrangements to induce docility, not economic independence, among their tenants. Only cooperative tenants who paid their rents regularly and in full could expect to benefit. And once tenants did have a little land of their own, landlords believed they would become more "conservative," grateful to their landlords and uninterested in protest movements.[50]

By means of these and other measures landlords were able in some cases, no doubt, to offset the advantages tenants enjoyed in disputes. But neither combat nor preemption succeeded in reversing established trends. The number of tenancy disputes declined after 1926, it is true, but the decrease was slight. More important, as in the early 1920s, at the end of the decade compromise settlements prevailed.

It was clear to contemporary observers that major obstacles existed to effective resistance by landlords to their tenants' demands. Landlord unions, in particular, tended to be short-lived,[51] suggesting that differences among their members were simply too great to allow sustained collaboration. Indeed, in most rural communities landlords were more divided by differences than united by the common activity of leasing land. Old landed families tended to be jealous of the wealth of the *nouveau riche*; resident landlords were contemptuous of absentee landlords who escaped the burden of local taxes. The greatest differences, of course, stemmed from the size of landlords' holdings. Large landlords could more easily

49. *Okayama ken kosaku kankō chōsa sho,* p. 90.
50. Ibid.
51. Kyōchōkai, nōsonka, *Nōson shakai no dōkō* (Tokyo, 1932), pp. 71-72.

absorb rent reductions than could small landlords; or, because of their accumulated reserves of rice, they could afford to hold out longer against tenant demands. Given their local influence and the large number of tenants to whom they rented land, they generally were able to determine landlord strategy in any given dispute.[52] Small landlords, and those who depended solely on rental income, often felt victimized not only by tenant militancy, but by the decisions of large landlords as well. These and other sources of friction among landlords made it possible for tenants to apply their strategy of divide-and-conquer with continued success.

The inability of landlords to mount effective resistance in disputes obviously exacted an economic toll. Landlords found not only their rental income but also the value of their land holdings reduced after disputes. In one part of Yamanashi Prefecture, for example, rents on rice paddy fell by 15 percent as the result of a series of disputes; the price of paddy, however, fell by 25 percent.[53]

Although more difficult to document, disputes undoubtedly exacted a psychological toll on landlords as well. In place of the security they had enjoyed in the past, landlords now experienced fairly constant uncertainty. They had no assurance that rents would be forthcoming in any given year or that, in the aftermath of one dispute, new demands for further rent reductions would not be made in the near future. For large landlords this uncertainty may have been only a minor irritation. But for the vast majority of smaller landlords it must have been a source of considerable anxiety.

Conflict itself, and especially unsuccessful conflict, must have been damaging to the self-esteem of landlords whatever the size of

52. Arimoto Hideo, "Jinushi wa onozukara kamen o dasseyo," *Nōsei kenkyū* 3 (1924): 27–28; see also Nōrinshō, nōmukyoku, *Kosaku sōgi no gaikyō* (Tokyo, 1928), pp. 14–15.
53. Okutani Matsuji, *Kindai Nihon nōsei shiron* (Tokyo, 1938), pp. 218–19. See also Nagahara Keiji et al., *Nihon jinushi sei no kōsei to dantai* (Tokyo, 1972), p. 271, for additional data from Yamanashi showing that land values in seven villages declined 7 to 40 percent in the immediate aftermath of disputes. Dore, too, implies a causal relationship between tenant unrest and declining land values. See Ronald Dore, *Land Reform in Japan* (London, 1959), pp. 21–22.

their holdings. No longer did they enjoy unquestioned authority in their communities; rather, their decisions were regularly challenged by tenants, and at times they were subjected to indignities unheard of in the past. Tenants would snub them on the village streets, or surround their houses late at night, chanting and beating on drums. In one village in Aichi Prefecture where a dispute was in progress, 500 tenants surrounded the temple in which local landlords were meeting to discuss strategy and kept the landlords imprisoned all night.[54] To the extent that one's social status is determined not simply by income or pedigree but also by how one is treated,[55] tenant militancy and disrespectful behavior—in short, the tenants' withdrawal of deference—surely came as a painful blow to landlords, undermining their self-confidence and leading them to question the merits of land ownership.

Nor were the problems landlords faced confined to the countryside. The appointment of Hara Satoshi as Prime Minister in 1918 marked the beginning of an assault on their interests at the national level as well. Although ultimately less damaging to landlords than tenancy disputes, this assault, too, exacted its toll.

Two steps initiated by the Hara government before the Prime Minister's assassination in 1921 were viewed by landlords as direct threats to their interests. The first was reform of existing policies concerning the supply and price of rice. Owing to population growth and a slow rise in personal income, especially among urban workers, the demand for rice had increased steadily since mid-Meiji. By the 1890s demand began to exceed domestic supply. Exports of rice were curtailed at this time, and the government began importing foreign rice (*gaimai*) to provide emergency food supplies. But despite these measures the domestic price of rice continued to rise.[56]

Because they received rents in kind, landlords profited handsomely from price increases. They were alarmed, however, by the

54. *Aichi ken nōchi shi* 1: 452–53.

55. A phenomenon discussed by Lawrence Stone in *Crisis of the Aristocracy* (London, 1967), pp. 349–54.

56. *Nihon nōmin undō shi,* p. 402; see also Tōbata Seiichi, "Nihon nōgyō hatten no ninaite," in Nōgyō hattatsu shi chōsa kai, ed., *Nihon nōgyō hattatsu shi* 9:595–96.

growing magnitude of rice imports after the turn of the century. When the government announced plans in 1904 to raise land taxes as part of an emergency program to cover the costs of the Russo-Japanese War, landed interests in the Diet demanded a protective tariff on rice imports in exchange. Unable or unwilling to contest this demand, the government agreed to a 15 percent duty. When the war ended a year later the same landed interests, backed by the Imperial Agricultural Association, refused to allow repeal of the duty. In 1911 they succeeded in raising tariffs on rice and other imported grains and in making protection of domestic agriculture an official policy of the government. Although shortages of rice frequently arose in succeeding years, in response to pressure from landlords the government did little to encourage rice cultivation in either Taiwan or Korea, Japan's colonial possessions.[57]

By the end of World War I, however, the situation had changed radically. The Rice Riots of 1918, in which thousands of Japanese had taken to the streets, revealed the extent of popular discontent with rising rice prices. The representatives of commercial and industrial interests in the Diet, too, demanded a cheap and abundant supply of rice as a means of maintaining existing wages levels and, hence, of promoting the nation's ability to sell goods abroad.[58] On the basis of its failure to devise effective means of controlling prices, the Terauchi government had been forced to resign. Hara recognized as he assumed office that unless he was more successful, his government would suffer the same fate.

Although Hara's party, the Seiyukai, has been described as a bastion of landed interests throughout the prewar decades, landlords and their allies in the Diet proved unable to prevent a change in the policy they had championed for over fifteen years. By means of the Rice Law of 1920, enacted with the support of business interests in both the Seiyukai and Kenseikai, duties on foreign rice were removed and a program for developing rice cultivation in

57. Ibid., pp. 596–99; *Nihon nōmin undō shi,* pp. 402–4; Okutani, pp. 175–76.
58. *Nihon nōmin undō shi,* pp. 276–77; Tōbata, "Nihon nōgyō hatten no ninaite," pp. 600–602.

Taiwan and Korea was initiated. In addition, a system of price controls on rice was established, marking a first step in the government's abandonment of its long-standing policy of laissez faire toward agricultural prices.[59]

Landlords were alarmed not only by this change in policy, but also by the ease with which it had been effected. It seemed to many that their political influence was in serious jeopardy. Already it had been noted in the journal of the Imperial Agricultural Association that the representation of landlords among the nation's highest taxpayers in the House of Peers had declined from 49 percent in 1890 to 29 percent in 1918. Now attention was called to the erosion of landlord strength in the House of Representatives as well: in the 1890s landlords had constituted over 50 percent of all representatives, but in 1920 they constituted only 20 percent.[60] Whether these figures actually demonstrated declining landlord political influence is, of course, open to question. After all, a Diet member did not necessarily have to be a landlord himself to support legislation favorable to landlords. But landlords were nonetheless concerned. In the face of continuing urbanization, industrial development and reductions in property qualifications for voting, they did not regard increasing their influence in the Diet as an easy matter.

The second step taken by the Hara government was the creation in 1920 of a research committee, headed by Minister of Agriculture Yamamoto Tatsuo, to study possible reform of the tenancy system. At the first general meeting of the committee Yamamoto stated:

The Civil Code defines the rights and obligations of landlords and tenants in a general way. But in actual practice, their relations are based on long-standing customs which vary greatly throughout the country. . . . Under these diverse customs the number of tenant farmers [including both landless tenants and tenants who owned some land of their own] has increased to almost 70 percent of total farm households. . . . Thus, the tenancy system

59. Ibid.
60. "Kizokuin tagaku nōzeisha giin gosensha ni tsuite," *Teikoku nōkai hō* 8 (July 1919): 60–61; Yamada Ken, "Sōsenkyo ni taisuru nōgyōsha no kakugo," *Teikoku nōkai hō* 20 (April 1920): 9.

affects not only the interests of landlords and tenants, but also of agriculture and rural society as a whole. The greatest defect of the tenancy system is that it sometimes provokes disputes between landlords and tenants. These disputes are not simply a local problem, but a grave matter for our whole society. The recent growth of industry and commerce, the shortage of agricultural labor, and the rise in prices and the cost of living have also influenced landlord-tenant relations. The tendency for various ideologies to spread from the cities to the countryside is particularly alarming. We urgently need to reform the tenancy system.[61]

Like most government officials, Yamamoto was alarmed by the spread of "urban ideologies" to rural areas. Yet he did not regard these ideologies as the basic cause of disputes. Instead he blamed, rather vaguely to be sure, the defects of the tenancy system itself. He recognized that the Civil Code provided an inadequate legal basis for landlord-tenant relations; citing the rapid growth of tenancy since early Meiji, which had made tenancy disputes a matter of grave concern for the nation as a whole, he advocated government action in reforming the tenancy system. Thus, just as the Hara government showed signs of abandoning laissez faire toward rice prices, it now threatened to abandon its long-standing policy of non-intervention in tenancy relations.

As noted previously, the Civil Code of 1898 had imposed few restrictions on the ownership rights of landlords. If tenanted land was sold, the new owner was under no compulsion to recognize or retain existing tenants. Moreover, the maximum duration permitted ordinary tenancy rights was twenty years; no minimum time limit was established. As a result, landlords could cancel tenancy agreements at any time. Tenants were not allowed to sublet or transfer tenancy rights without their landlord's consent. If, owing to unavoidable circumstances, the yield on leased land fell below the level of rents, tenants had the right to demand that rents be reduced to the amount of yield—a "right" which would leave them with absolutely nothing when harvests were poor. Of course, landlords

61. "Kosaku seido chōsa iinkai," *Teikoku nōkai hō* 10 (December 1920): 60-61.

were constrained by custom to reduce rents whenever harvests fell below normal and to leave their tenants with at least part of the crop. But if they refused to do so, tenants had no legal grounds for complaint.[62] In effect, then, the economic security of tenants was outside the realm of law.

The first step taken by Yamamoto's research committee was discussion of a draft tenancy law which established legal guarantees for the economic security of tenants. In so doing, the draft imposed a number of important restrictions on the ownership rights of landlords, eliminating most of the legal and customary advantages they had enjoyed over their tenants since the Restoration. As one proponent of the draft put it:

It is not enough simply to draft a law which will put a stop to tenancy disputes. Hitherto the whole system has been too unfavorable to the tenant, and our object should be to attempt, in a new spirit and as a matter of social justice, to remove the root causes of disputes.[63]

According to the draft, ordinary tenancy was recognized as a right which could be bought and sold without the landlord's consent. A minimum duration of fifteen years was imposed on such rights. At the end of that time, the tenant could demand renewal of tenancy on the same terms which had existed in the past. His landlord's ability to refuse was closely circumscribed. If the tenant had failed to pay rents for a specified number of years or had damaged the land he cultivated, the landlord could petition his local tenancy commission, a judicial body to be especially created to deal with landlord-tenant conflict, for permission to terminate the agreement. Or, if he wanted to farm the land himself or use it for some other purpose "serving the public interest," he could buy existing tenancy rights at a fair price. He could not, however, evict one tenant merely to replace him with another. If tenancy was terminated, the tenant was entitled to compensation for any improvements he had made on the land.

62. Ogura, *Tochi rippō*, p. 221; Dore, *Land Reform*, pp. 64–65.
63. Yahagi Eizō, professor of agricultural policy at Tokyo Imperial University, quoted in Dore, *Land Reform*, p. 81.

In addition, the draft provided that under certain circumstances a tenant could elect to pay his rent in cash or in interest-free installments. If yield fell below the level of rent, he could demand a rent reduction which would leave him with enough of the crop to provide for his food supply and the costs of farming during the following year. Both landlords and tenants could petition their local tenancy commission to determine fair rent levels. Once a fair rent had been established, it could not be changed for at least five years and then only with the commission's approval. In a subsequent revision of the draft, both permanent and ordinary tenants were granted prior rights of purchase if their landlords decided to sell their land.[64]

Having suffered defeat on the issue of rice prices, landlords were determined to prevent action on the proposed tenancy law. And despite their reduced numbers in the Diet they were able to do so successfully. One reason was their representation on the research committee itself, which gave them a forum for expressing their views and an opportunity to delay and complicate debate on the draft. Of thirty-one participants on the committee, twelve were Diet members, six from each house. All but one of the representatives from the House of Peers were landlords owning 100 *chō* or more. Two of the six representatives from the lower house owned over 90 *chō* of land. The holdings of the remaining four are not known, but since they were all active in agricultural affairs, typically as high-ranking officials in the Imperial Agricultural Association, it is probable that they, too, owned land. The rest of the committee was composed of bureaucrats and scholars, several of whom sided with the landed members. There were no representatives of tenant farmers.[65]

A second reason for the success of landlords in preventing action on the draft tenancy law was the well-organized and persistent

64. Ogura, *Tochi rippō,* pp. 325–29, 335.
65. "Kosaku seido chōsa iinkai," p. 60. The five landed Peers were Hoshijima Gihei (Okayama, 125 *chō*), Yaguchi Chōzaemon (Tochigi, 125 *chō*), Yamada Ken (Fukui, 140 *chō*), Sato Yuzaemon (Niigata, 523 *chō*), and Hosokawa Moritatsu, a marquis and member of a former daimyo family. Among the representatives from the lower house, Matsuda Minoru (Kagawa) owned 94 *chō* and Koshio Hachirozaemon (Kanagawa) owned 96 *chō*.

lobbying of landlord unions. Even before the committee had completed its deliberations a version of the proposed law was published in major newspapers, arousing a storm of protest from landlord unions throughout the country. The petition submitted to the committee by the Gifu Landlords' Association in 1921 was typical of the position these unions took toward the law. In its preface the petition observed:

The aim of the draft is to facilitate the peaceful development of agriculture by restraining those landlords who are high-handed [in their dealings with tenants], by protecting tenants, and by settling disputes between the two groups. However, its provisions are too harsh on landlords as a whole. Too many obligations are placed on them. As a result, we fear that they will lose their paternalistic feeling toward their tenants and abandon interest in improving their land. Moreover, the draft has no provisions . . . to control insincere or dishonest activity by tenants. It is clear that the proposed law will lead to even more disputes and invite the ruin of agriculture.[66]

Then the petition recommended the elimination or emasculation of almost every measure designed to protect tenants, in effect advocating the maintenance of the legal framework for tenancy relations provided by the Civil Code.[67]

In addition to petitioning the research committee, the landlord unions also circulated statements explaining their opposition to the proposed law among all members of the Diet and sent delegations to Tokyo to present their views in person to influential politicians. Two themes were constantly reiterated: 1) the law was an undue invasion of private property rights, and 2) it would encourage, rather than discourage, the spread both of "subversive" ideologies among tenant farmers and of disputes themselves.[68]

To increase their influence the unions began organizing regional federations. The most notable example was the Japan Landlords' Association founded in Osaka in the mid-1920s. By 1928 it claimed 10,000 members, most of them small landlords from southwestern

66. Quoted in Ogura, *Tochi rippō*, p. 345.
67. Ibid., pp. 346–49.
68. *Nōchi kaikaku tenmatsu gaiyō*, p. 69.

Japan. Arguing that the proposed law would ruin small landlords, the Association prepared its own list of amendments, which, like those of the Gifu Landlords' Association, amounted to little more than a reaffirmation of the Civil Code. Tenancy was to remain an obligation (*saiken*), its minimum duration reduced from fifteen to three years. All proposed restrictions on the cancellation of tenancy or the sale of tenanted land were removed. Instead of a right to rent reductions when harvests were poor, tenants were granted the right to negotiate (individually, not collectively) for reductions, a provision even more limited than that of the Civil Code itself.[69]

Confronted by vociferous and unyielding opposition from landlord unions, the research committee was forced to abandon discussion of the tenancy law. A proposal for recognizing the right of tenants to form unions and bargain collectively was also shelved. Although several attempts were made subsequently to revive both proposals, each time the landlord unions reacted with a well-organized campaign in opposition.

Only two laws dealing directly with tenancy were passed during the 1920s, neither of them posing a serious threat to landed interests. The first was the Tenancy Conciliation Law of 1924, designed to settle, not prevent, disputes. It provided for the voluntary submission of disputes to local conciliation committees headed by a district magistrate with two or more members selected by the magistrate from lists prepared by the chief of the district court. Those appearing on these lists were usually prefectural assemblymen, village mayors, or other "men of local influence." The only law on which these committees could base their decisions, of course, was the Civil Code which favored landlords over tenants.[70]

The second law was the Regulations for the Establishment of Owner-Cultivators, enacted in 1926. These regulations provided for loans to tenant farmers, at 3.5 percent for twenty-five years, to

---

69. Ogura, *Tochi rippō,* pp. 465–76 passim.
70. Ibid., pp. 346–49. I have been unable to determine how many disputes were submitted to formal conciliation, however, or if the committees actually favored landlords in the decisions they reached.

enable them to buy land—if they could find someone willing to sell. The program itself was limited in scope and would have transferred ownership of only 4 percent of all tenanted land in the nation had it been carried out to the full extent of its funding. Moreover, it enabled landlords to practice in an organized fashion what some of them had been doing privately for years: selling tenants tiny plots of land—and the promise, albeit remote, of eventual elevation into the ranks of owner-cultivators—in order to promote their loyalty and obedience.[71] Finally, since a large portion, estimated at 50 percent, of all land acquired by tenants under these regulations was located in Hokkaido,[72] the program may well have served as a conduit for the removal of the most disaffected and troublesome tenants from the rural areas of other major islands of the country.

Landlords managed, then, to withstand the political assault on their interests fairly well. But I do not believe they were able, in the late 1920s, to take much comfort in their accomplishments. They had failed, after all, to prevent passage of the Rice Law. Once the dominant group within the Diet, able to wield direct influence on decision making, they now felt themselves a minority, forced to rely heavily on petitioning and lobbying. And they still experienced the uncertainty and economic loss brought about by tenancy disputes.

In the late 1920s some landlords redoubled their efforts to destroy the tenant movement, usually by advocating local legislation to outlaw collective bargaining and boycotts, two of the most potent weapons of tenant unions.[73] But for other landlords, the effect of disputes on income and the value of land was the last straw. Convinced that the re-establishment of peaceful tenancy relations would require greater economic sacrifices than they were prepared to make and aware of the profitability and relative security of other forms of investment, they began to liquidate their holdings.

71. Dore, *Land Reform*, pp. 83–84.
72. Supreme Commander Allied Powers, Natural Resources Section, *Tenancy in Japan* (Tokyo, 1947), p. 33.
73. Dore, *Land Reform*, pp. 84–85.

124

Between 1922 and 1945 large absentee landlords sold over 550 *chō* in one village in southern Okayama Prefecture, most of it to their tenants and local owner-cultivators.[74] Landlords in Aichi, Gumma and Niigata Prefectures used proceeds from the sale of their property to invest in farmland in Korea where tenancy disputes were extremely rare.[75] Of five landlords owning 10 *chō* or more surveyed by Saitō Eiichi in 1932, only one purchased land after 1927. Three sold portions of their holdings and invested more heavily in stocks and bonds. The fifth, concerned about tenancy disputes in his own and neighboring villages, decided not to acquire any more land.[76] Although admittedly a small sample, Saitō's findings were probably fairly representative, at least of larger landlords.

Perhaps the most dramatic reaction of landlords to tenancy disputes occurred in 1927. In that year a group of landlords in the House of Peers, acting with the support of the Japan Landlords' Association, issued three alternative proposals for land reform. The first called for the nationalization of all land in Japan, rural and urban. In place of private land ownership, the state would serve as a national landlord, leasing land to farmers, businessmen and city dwellers at fair rents. The second called for the nationalization of arable land only, which would then be rented out in compact parcels to farmers. The third was still narrower in scope. Only tenanted farmland would be acquired by the state. If a tenant wanted to buy the land he tilled, he could do so at the price the state had paid for it. If an owner-cultivator wanted to sell land, he could sell only to another cultivator or to the state. No private individual would be allowed to lease arable land to others or to own land which he did not cultivate. All three proposals provided that the state would purchase land from its present owners at current market prices.[77]

74. Yoshioka Kin'ichi, *Kindaiteki nōson no rekishi to jittai* (Tokyo, 1951), p. 62.
75. Asada Kyōji, "Kōtaiki Nihon jinushi sei no sonzai keitai," *Tochi seido shigaku*, No. 34 (January 1967), p. 10.
76. Saitō Eiichi, "Jinushi no zaisan kōsei ni tsuite," part 1, *Shakai seisaku jihō* No. 156 (September 1933), pp. 71, 76.
77. Kitazaki Susumu, "Tochi kokuyūan no kachi," *Chūgai zaikai* 2 (1927): 52; Dorothy Orchard, "Agrarian Problems of Modern Japan," part 2, *Journal of*

As a contemporary observer noted: "One expects to hear such proposals from the socialists. To have them made by the landlords themselves is truly remarkable."[78] Indeed, considering the opposition of many of these same landlords, both in the House of Peers and in the Japan Landlords' Association, to earlier attempts to reform the tenancy system—often on the grounds that proposed legislation violated private property rights—these proposals do seem strange. Yet there was a vital difference, as far as landlords were concerned, between tenancy reform and land reform. Tenancy reform, as envisioned by Yamamoto's research committee, would make an already insecure form of investment even more precarious. No longer would landlords be able to terminate tenancy agreements at will or to raise rents freely. And although many of the advantages of leasing land would be lost, the obligations—paying taxes, for example—would remain. Land reform, on the other hand, offered complete escape from what they considered a rapidly deteriorating situation. With the money they received for their land former landlords could establish businesses or invest in the stock market, clipping coupons peacefully instead of contending with tenancy disputes.

There was, then, nothing contradictory in the stance of landlords on these two issues. Both stemmed from the calculation of their own self-interest. If possible, they wanted to preserve the status quo in tenancy relations—or more accurately, the state of affairs which had existed before World War I. Hence their opposition to tenancy reform. But if that proved impossible—and by the late 1920s it seemed to many landlords that tenants were gaining ground even without the assistance of legislation—they preferred to give up their

---

Political Economy 37 (June 1929): 308. The proposals generated a brief flurry of comment, but were never formally presented to the House of Peers. A substitute plan proposed to the cabinet by the Minister of Agriculture later in 1927, which called for government acquisition of 800,000 *chō* of tenanted land over a thirty-five-year period, was opposed by the Home and Finance Ministers, tabled until the 1928 Diet session, and never reconsidered.

78. Kitazaki, p. 52.

land on the most advantageous terms they could secure rather than endure further erosion of their position. There were limits, however, to what they could accomplish on their own: although many farmers wanted land, few could afford to buy substantial parcels. Landlords saw a government-sponsored program of land reform as the only viable solution.

Had these proposals been sponsored by landed Peers alone one might conclude that they represented the thinking of large landlords only. But support by the Japan Landlords' Association, spokesman for smaller landlords, suggests the idea of reform had considerably wider appeal. If the Great Depression had not struck Japan two years later, it is possible that some kind of reform—most probably of tenanted farmland only—would have been enacted. After all, it was not just a small group of officials in the Ministry of Agriculture and the leaders of the tenant movement who supported the idea; so did many owners of tenanted land.

But the Depression made reform impossible for several reasons. First, the government was no longer in a position to assume the financial burden which land reform entailed. Second, because land values had plummeted in response to falling agricultural prices, few landlords remained willing to sell their holdings. Third, the very attractiveness of other forms of investment had been thrown into question by the collapse of the stock market, the closing of many banks, and widespread business failures. One might not make money from owning land, but at least one had food to eat. Growing support for land reform among landlords temporarily evaporated, therefore, as the future of the whole economy, not just of agriculture, became uncertain. By the time the economy began to recover, the government was too concerned about developments on the Asian continent and the threat of war to consider land reform again.

Landlord-Tenant Conflict, 1932–1941

The spread of disputes to the Tohoku and other outlying regions of the country in the 1930s cannot be attributed to the appearance there of the "mood of tenant militancy" that had affected the Kinki and Chubu in the 1920s.[79] Instead, most of the disputes in these regions, and a substantial portion of all disputes in the country in the 1930s, were caused by the economic distress of landlords during the Depression.

The Depression had a profound impact on Japanese agriculture. With the collapse of the American silk market, the price of silk cocoons in Japan fell by over 60 percent. As domestic industrial production slackened, moreover, consumer demand for agricultural produce declined. A bumper rice harvest in 1930 and increasing imports of rice from Taiwan and Korea, the result of the colonial development program begun in the early 1920s, compounded the problem. Rice prices fell to 18.6 yen per *koku* in 1931, the lowest since 1916, outstripping the fall in price of other consumer goods. Prices for many fruits and vegetables, luxuries for most Japanese, fell even more sharply.[80]

As a result of the Depression, thousands of unemployed urban workers returned to their native villages, their train fare paid by the government as a social relief measure.[81] With a surplus of idle labor in almost every village and many families eager to lease land on even the most unfavorable terms, it became increasingly risky for tenants to initiate disputes. That disputes increased in number nonetheless was due in large part to the actions of their landlords.

With the sudden decline in agricultural prices, the incomes landlords received from the sale of rent rice were sharply reduced, although the land taxes they paid remained essentially unchanged. Large landlords, who had been able to accumulate reserves of rice and money during prosperous years, simply reduced unnecessary expenses, but many small landlords, especially those owning less than 1 *chō* of land, found themselves in desperate straits. Their

79. As Ronald Dore and Tsutomu Ōuchi assert in "Rural Origins of Japanese Fascism," in *Dilemmas of Growth in Prewar Japan,* ed. James Morley, (Princeton, 1971), p. 184.

80. Dore, *Land Reform,* pp. 87–88; *Nihon nōmin undō shi,* pp. 125–26; Nōrinshō, nōmukyoku, *Chihō betsu kosaku sōgi gaiyō* 2 (Tokyo, 1936): 476.

81. Dore, *Land Reform,* p. 88.

savings, if any, were modest, and their reserves of rice minimal at best. Like their tenants, many had obtained part-time jobs in nearby towns. Now, however, they found themselves laid off and in many cases called upon to house and feed relatives who had returned home from the cities. Only with difficulty could they maintain their already frugal way of life. Frequently, they were concerned about having enough to eat.[82]

There were three principal ways in which these smaller landlords tried to alleviate their distress, all of which led directly or indirectly to tenancy disputes. One was to take advantage of the increased competition for land among tenant farmers, canceling existing tenancy agreements and leasing their fields at substantially higher rents to new tenants—typically, to farmers who had relied heavily on wage earnings in the past and were now desperately in need of additional land.[83] The second was to resume farming themselves or to expand the area of land they already cultivated by evicting some tenants totally or by taking back a *tan* or two of land from several of them.[84] By eliminating the tenants' share of the crop they were assured of their own food supply; if harvests were good they could sell even more rice than before, compensating at least partially for the decline in prices. The third way was to sell small parcels of their land. In most cases, however, prospective buyers wanted to farm the land themselves and ordered current tenants to abandon it.[85] In all three cases the threatened tenants, also hard-pressed economically, were apt to protest, demanding that they be allowed to continue cultivation.[86]

82. All the landlords surveyed by Saitō Eiichi in the early 1930s had mortgaged at least part of their land to banks or other financial institutions. "Zaisan kōsei," part 1, pp. 76–77.

83. See *Chihō betsu kosaku sōgi gaiyō* 2: 55 (Miyagi); 3: 49 (Miyagi); 78 (Yamagata).

84. Ibid., pp. 45–46 (Miyagi); 77–78 (Yamagata); 2: 49 (Iwate).

85. Ibid., pp. 36–37 (Aomori); 49 (Iwate); 3: 76–77 (Yamagata). For a case study of a dispute arising from the sale of tenanted land, see Nōrinshō, nōmukyoku, *Kosaku sōgi oyobi chōtei jirei* 9 (Tokyo, 1936): 252–54.

86. Not all attempted evictions led to disputes. In many cases, tenants feared losing whatever land they still retained and acquiesced quietly to landlord demands. Okada Munemori, "Saikin ni okeru kosaku sōgi no jōkyō to nōmin kumiai undō

As noted previously, disputes triggered by attempted evictions were especially numerous in the Tohoku. These disputes, like those in central Honshu earlier, were also the product of the specific circumstances prevailing in the region. Unlike disputes in central Honshu, however, those in the Tohoku were caused not by economic development and the dissociation of landlords from rural life, but by their very opposites.

During the 1920s the economic backwardness of the Tohoku had served as a check on the outbreak of tenancy disputes. There were far fewer opportunities than in the Kinki or Chubu regions for tenants to obtain part-time employment outside of agriculture. If they did have off-season work, it was more likely to be in fishing or handicraft production, which did not provide them with much income, than in industry. As a result, they remained more dependent on farming and less aware of its economic disadvantages.[87] True, tenants in the Tohoku had access to information about tenancy disputes in other parts of the country. As one northern landlord remarked after a series of disputes in Gifu Prefecture:

One must take note of the newspapers. . . . If there is any sort of incident they speedily report it. In some ways, this is admirable, but it also gives evil knowledge to farmers who themselves know nothing of such things.[88]

Moreover, university students in the Tohoku, following the example set by young activists from Tokyo in the early 1920s, made numerous

---

no dōkō," part 1. *Teikoku nōkai hō* 26 (June 1936), pp. 57–58. Okada also notes that a different kind of eviction dispute had occurred in the 1920s. Then landlords used evictions primarily to discourage tenant participation in unions. After the enactment of universal manhood suffrage in 1925, moreover, some landlords told their tenants how to vote, threatening to evict those who refused to comply. Ibid., p. 57.

87. The farm population of Yamagata Prefecture, one of the most prosperous in the Tohoku, actually increased between 1907 and 1938, causing a reduction of slightly more than 1 *tan* in the area of land per farm household. See Yamagata ken keizaibu, *Kosaku jijō to nōmin undō* (Yamagata, 1940), p. 1. With greater population pressure on the land, the ability of tenant farmers to wage disputes was not very great.

88. Niigata ken nōkai, ed., *Jinushi kosaku mondai ni taisuru jinushi no iken* (Niigata, 1921), p. 27.

attempts to organize local tenant unions and political parties.[89] But neither the mass media nor the student movement had much impact on tenants.

One important reason, other than the traditionalism of the tenants themselves, was the continued traditionalism of their landlords, which also had its basis in the economic backwardness of the region. Unlike central Honshu, the Tohoku contained few large cities to entice landlords away from their native villages and fewer investment opportunities, locally at least, to attract their capital from agriculture. A larger percentage of landlords than in central Honshu, therefore, remained in the countryside as resident landlords, living unostentatiously as a rule, cultivating some of their land themselves, and taking an active interest in local affairs.[90] It is likely that many tenants envied, and perhaps resented, their higher standard of living—the first thing tenants in one village did after the postwar land reform was to add new baths and toilets to their homes similar to those their landlords had built in the 1920s.[91] But overt hostility was rare, largely because most landlords continued to perform their traditional role in village society. The very presence of landlords in the villages, and the frequency of their personal contacts with tenants, militated against the open expression of conflict.

89. Sunaga, *Kindai Nihon no jinushi,* pp. 357-58.
90. One example were the Otaki of Yamagata Prefecture, who owned 164 *chō* of land in the 1920s and farmed 3 *chō* themselves. Although they were wealthy, they lived simply, mixing barley with their rice as an example of frugality to their tenants. Only one member of the family received more than a middle school education, and apart from financing an abortive silk-reeling venture, they took little interest in commercial affairs. Instead, their goal was to preserve and extend the family land holdings. The rents the Otaki charged were some 10 percent higher than the amount they expected to collect. Thus, they were able to grant rent reductions every year, even when the harvest was normal, as a means of demonstrating their "generosity." After rents were collected, they held a feast for all their tenants. They provided clothing and utensils for local weddings and contributed money for village festivals. Because they displayed benevolence and made no attempt to dissociate themselves from village life, they enjoyed harmonious relations with their tenants. They were never involved in disputes. Dore, *Land Reform,* pp. 30-41. See also KS 2: 278 (Yamagata); 383 (Akita).
91. Interview with Ueno Kyō, mayor of Nango village and former landlord, Miyagi Prefecture, 27 May 1967.

During the 1930s, however, the economic backwardness of the Tohoku and the traditionalism of its landlords made tenancy disputes more likely than elsewhere in the nation. Because of its harsh climate, poor harvests were still fairly common in the region, their impact intensified by the impossibility of double-cropping. Few but the largest landlords had substantial savings; what little money they did possess was usually deposited in small provincial banks, many of which failed in the early months of the Depression.[92] Forced to sell more rice than before to pay taxes, landlords could no longer tolerate rent arrears or grant generous rent reductions when crops were poor. A non-cultivating, absentee landlord in the Kinki or Chubu who found himself in similar straits might well hesitate before demanding part of his land back for farming; if, after all, he proved unsuccessful at raising crops he would end up with no income at all. But many landlords in the Tohoku, precisely because they were experienced farmers, owned all the necessary tools, and were well acquainted with local farming conditions, thought immediately of expanding the area of land they cultivated as a way out of their predicament. The same characteristics which had marked them as "good" landlords in the past now generated disputes.

Moreover, it appears that economic recovery from the Depression was slower in the Tohoku than in the Kinki or Chubu. In Osaka, for example, expansion of the munitions industry after the Manchurian Incident of 1931 and successful efforts to promote foreign trade contributed to an early return to prosperity.[93] Demand for agricultural produce rose again as workers resumed their jobs, bringing about an upswing in prices for rice and other crops.[94] Once again landlords could profit from the sale of rent rice, and the investments they had made outside the agricultural sector once more yielded dividends.

92. See *Chihō betsu kosaku sōgi gaiyō* 3: 13 (Aomori).
93. Ibid., p. 401.
94. After 1932 rice prices on the Osaka exchange were higher than prices on the Tokyo exchange. Nōrinshō, nōmukyoku, *Honpō nōgyō yōran* (Tokyo, 1940), pp. 226-27.

But there was little industry in the Tohoku capable of playing such a role. A number of large landlords sponsored public works projects in their villages—one landlord in Miyagi Prefecture donated over 400,000 yen between 1929 and 1933 for the construction of local roads, a bridge, telephone exchange, and post office[95]—but on the whole their efforts provided only temporary relief and did little to provide a basis for economic recovery. The economic problems faced by landlords in the Tohoku, therefore, if not more severe to begin with certainly were more long-lasting. Contemporary official reports on tenancy conditions in the Kinki and Chubu make only brief mention of the distress of landlords. But similar reports from the Tohoku dwell at length on their difficulties and note an increasing trend in the mid-1930s toward sales of tenanted land by smaller landlords, either privately or by public auction, as a means of raising cash for basic living expenses, taxes, or the repayment of debts.[96] Since those who bought land at this time usually wanted to farm it themselves, these sales led to a new wave of eviction disputes.

As in the 1920s, most disputes in the 1930s ended in compromise settlements (Table 17).[97] Owing to the different nature of disputes, however, compromise did not have the same significance now as earlier. In fact, since most disputes involved attempts at eviction, compromise tended to favor landlords. They might consent to let tenants continue cultivating the disputed fields for an additional year instead of evicting them immediately, or they might provide tenants with only token compensation for the loss of cultivating rights. In most cases, tenants were deprived in some measure of their livelihood, and landlords were free, sooner or later, to use the land they repossessed to their own advantage. Although landlords rarely were able to solve the economic problems they faced by evicting tenants, they were able to ease their distress somewhat.

95. Sunaga, *Kindai Nihon no jinushi*, pp. 378-80.
96. See *Chihō betsu kosaku sōgi gaiyō* 3:13-14 (Aomori); 45-48 (Miyagi); 77-78 (Yamagata).
97. As shown in Table 17, tenants appear to have won an unusually high percentage of disputes between 1930 and 1934, a fact for which I have uncovered no satisfactory explanation.

Landlords also made political gains in the 1930s. Their representation in the Diet continued to decline, but they made up for what
they lacked in numbers by the volume and frequency of their statements about the plight of agriculture and their protests against
existing government policies. Their main target was the program of
colonial agricultural development launched in 1920.

Imports of colonial rice accounted for roughly 30 percent of all
rice sold on the domestic market in the early 1930s. Its volume, the
landlords argued, depressed domestic prices, causing rural distress.
Its very presence on the market was a threat to Japanese agriculture
and the millions of Japanese who made their livings from farming.
Asserting once more, as they had done during and immediately after
the Russo-Japanese War, that a nation facing troubled times must
be self-sufficient in food, they demanded renewed restrictions on
rice imports.

Here they gained an important ally, the Japanese military, which
was concerned both about the ability of the nation to feed itself
in wartime and about the health of its rural conscripts. Working
together, the landlords and the military were able to achieve a
reversal of government policy. The colonial development program
was abandoned, and imports of rice from Taiwan and Korea sharply
curtailed.[98]

98. Tōbata Seiichi, *Nihon shihonshugi no keisei sha* (Tokyo, 1964), pp. 144-45;
by the same author, "Nihon nōgyō hatten no ninaite," p. 603.

CHAPTER SIX

Conclusion

Tenancy disputes declined steadily in number in the early 1940s, following the outbreak of the Pacific War and the declaration of a national emergency. After more than two decades of conflict, peace—or at least a façade of peace—was restored to much of the countryside.[1] But the war itself, and the "China Incident" which preceded it, only exacerbated the problems of landlords. Although they no longer had to contend with tenant militancy or with economic depression, they now found themselves confronted by an even more powerful force, the Japanese government.

As part of a series of anti-inflationary measures, the government issued the Rent Control Order of 1939, which froze agricultural rents at their current levels and empowered local officials to order rent reductions if necessary.[2] Under the Staple Food Management Law of 1942, all rice was to be delivered to government warehouses, paid for by the government at officially determined prices, and

1. There were 2,756 disputes reported in 1942, 2,424 in 1943, and 2,160 in 1944, the last year for which figures are available. Nōchi seido shiryō shūsei hensan iinkai, *Kosaku sōgi ni kansuru shiryō* (Tokyo, 1969), pp. 50-51. I have been unable to locate information on where these disputes occurred or what sort of issues they involved.

2. Ogura Takekazu, *Tochi rippō no shiteki kōsatsu* (Tokyo, 1951), pp. 720-32 passim; Ronald Dore, *Land Reform in Japan* (London, 1959), p. 112.

milled and distributed by government agencies. At the same time, as a means of encouraging greater agricultural productivity and maximum deliveries of rice to the official, not the black, market, the government established a system of bonuses to be paid to the actual producers of rice—that is, to owner-cultivators, who also received the official price for their rice, and to tenants. Landlords were paid by the government for the rent rice they or their tenants brought to the warehouses, but unless they also delivered rice which they themselves had grown, they received no bonus payments. At first the bonuses paid to rice producers were relatively modest. But as the war progressed the amount was increased, at a rate far exceeding increases in official rice prices. In 1941, for example, landlords received 44 yen, tenants 5 yen, and owner-cultivators 49 yen for each *koku* of rice sold to the government. In 1945, however, landlords received only 55 yen per *koku,* while tenants received 245 yen and owner-cultivators, 300 yen.[3]

These new measures eliminated the remaining economic advantages of leasing land. Rents in kind had, in effect, been converted into money rents, and despite wartime inflation they could not be raised. No longer could landlords profit from the sale of rice. No doubt many landlords were alarmed by the government's policies,[4] but given the state of emergency by which all its actions had been justified, they were unable to protest.

These wartime measures did indeed "establish a beachhead for the postwar land reform,"[5] but it should be noted, too, that the landlords themselves had helped to mobilize the troops and materiel for the "invasion." Although they may have been impotent bystanders during the war itself, in earlier decades they had played an active, albeit unwitting, role in undermining their own position.

3. Ibid., p. 114; Tōbata Seiichi, *Nihon shihonshugi no keisei sha* (Tokyo, 1964), p. 146.
4. Some landlords were unable to purchase enough rice for their own consumption with the small amount of money they had left after paying taxes. Yoshioka Kin'ichi, *Kindaiteki nōson no rekishi to jittai* (Tokyo, 1951), p. 63.
5. Tōbata, *Nihon shihonshugi no keisei sha,* p. 146.

Landlords throughout the country had concerned themselves with promoting agricultural improvements. They had experimented with new crops and planting techniques, provided part of the capital and leadership needed to carry out land adjustment and reclamation projects, and helped to establish higher standards of quality for rice, the nation's most important crop. But to the extent that these improvements brought tenants both increased economic security and a greater share of the harvest, their dependence on landlords—a major barrier to the open expression of grievances—was reduced.

Agricultural improvements had other unforeseen consequences as well. Rice inspection programs contributed to the weakening of the vertical ties uniting a landlord and his tenants by providing opportunities for contact among tenant farmers in a given region. Land adjustment projects convinced tenants of the value of agricultural improvement, but, by focusing their attention on the improvement of secondary crops, sharpened their awareness of the ways in which their own economic interests differed from those of landlords. As a result, relations between landlords and tenants became increasingly impersonal and strained.

Even more damaging to the landlords' position, however, was their growing involvement in non-agricultural affairs. By abandoning farming, investing or working in industrial and commercial enterprises, and departing for the towns and cities of Japan, landlords were, in one sense, responding positively to the new opportunities and new national goals of the post-Restoration era. But at the same time, by dissociating themselves from rural life, they were giving up the remaining bases of their elite status in the countryside. Whether absentee landlords in a geographical or a functional sense, they were no longer able to behave as their tenants expected or to perform their time-honored role in village life.

The involvement of landlords in non-agricultural affairs was pronounced in central Honshu and figured as one major cause of tenancy disputes there in the years after World War I. The tenants who launched these disputes were motivated not only by economic grievances, but also by a sense of betrayal. Their landlords had not simply given up the cotton work clothes of farmers for Western-style suits and bowler hats; they had forsaken their communities and their tenants as well. Although tenants were, once aroused, increasingly susceptible to radical ideology and notions of status equality, initially they were engaged in a basically conservative protest against the decline of their landlords' paternalism.

It is true, of course, that the more traditional landlords of northeastern Japan were not immune to tenancy disputes. But, as I have attempted to demonstrate, a radically different dynamic was at work. Most disputes in the Tohoku in the 1930s were launched not by tenants, but by landlords. They were a product, moreover, of continuity, not of change, in the landlords' way of life. These disputes undoubtedly caused resentment among those tenants who found themselves threatened with the loss of cultivating rights. But owing to the small scale of disputes in this period, relatively few tenants were so affected.[6] The vast majority remained content with, or at least resigned to, the status quo. Although their economic status certainly declined in the aftermath of the Depression, landlords in the Tohoku still retained considerable power and authority in tenancy relations.

Yet few Tohoku landlords were able to view the future optimistically. Even without the warnings of fortunetellers and even before the imposition of wartime controls on agricultural rents and prices, many realized that being a landlord now provided more problems than rewards. Some, like landlords in central Honshu earlier, began selling off their holdings voluntarily—not because of immediate economic necessity but because of their desire to avoid conflict and economic losses in the years ahead.[7] Others merely resigned them-

6. As noted previously, eviction disputes in the Tohoku generally involved only one or two tenants, a single landlord, and very little land.

7. Some shifted their holdings from arable to forest land; others purchased urban real estate. A very few, like the Itō of Niigata Prefecture, purchased Chinese and Japanese art treasures, which they correctly perceived as a much safer and rewarding form of investment. Interview with Itō Bunkichi, Somi, Niigata Prefecture, 10 August 1967.

selves to being overcome eventually by circumstances they could neither fully understand nor control.

On the whole, landlords throughout Japan offered little resistance to the postwar land reform. Indeed, many of them had come to accept the necessity of reform long before experiencing the trauma of defeat and occupation. They may have been unaware of their own role in bringing about the deterioration of their status and influence in the countryside, but they did perceive that there was no future in leasing land to tenant farmers.

Bibliography

I. Books and Monographs in Japanese,
Including Japanese Government Documents

Aichi ken nōchi shi hensen iinkai. *Aichi ken nōchi shi* [The History of Agricultural Land in Aichi Prefecture]. 2 vols. Nagoya, 1957.

Amano Fujio. *Nōson shakai mondai: jinushi to kosakunin* [Rural Social Problems: Landlords and Tenants]. Tokyo, 1920.

Chūō bukka tōsei kyōryoku kaigi. *Nihon ni okeru nōgyō keiei narabi ni tochi shoyū no hensen ni kansuru sankō shiryō* [Reference Materials Concerning Changes in Agricultural Management and Land Ownership in Japan]. Tokyo, 1943.

Ehime ken naimubu. *Beikoku kensa jisshi no kosaku mondai ni oyoboshitaru eikyō* [The Influence of the Establishment of Rice Inspection on the Tenancy Problem]. Matsuyama, 1932.

Furushima Toshio, *Nihon jinushi sei shi kenkyū* [An Historical Study of the Japanese Landlord System]. Tokyo, 1958.

Hirano Yoshitarō. *Nihon shihonshugi shakai no kikō* [The Structure of Japanese Capitalist Society]. Tokyo, 1934.

Kamagata Isao. *Yamagata ken inasaku shi* [The History of Rice Cultivation in Yamagata Prefecture]. Tokyo, 1953.

Kondō Yasuo. *Mura no kōzō* [Village Organization]. Tokyo, 1955.

Kyōchōkai, nōsonka. *Honpō saikin no shakai undō* [The Recent Social Movement in Japan]. Tokyo, 1930.

_____. *Kosaku mondai o chūshin ni mitaru nōmin shisō* [Farmers' Thoughts about the Tenancy Problem]. Tokyo, 1926.

141

————. *Kosaku sōgi chi ni okeru nōson jijō* [Rural Conditions in Regions of Tenancy Disputes]. Tokyo, 1934.

————. *Kosaku sōgi chi ni okeru nōson jijō no henka* [Changes in Rural Conditions in Regions of Tenancy Disputes]. Tokyo, 1928.

————. *Nōson shakai no dōkō* [Trends in Rural Society]. Tokyo, 1932.

Morita Shirō. *Jinushi keizai to chihō shihon* [Landlord Finances and Local Capital]. Tokyo, 1963.

Nagahara Keiji et al., eds. *Nihon jinushi sei no kōsei to dankai* [The Composition and Stages of the Japanese Landlord System]. Tokyo, 1972.

Nasu Shiroshi. *Shōnai tadokoro no nōgyō nōson oyobi seikatsu* [Agriculture, Villages and Daily Life in the Shōnai Region]. Tokyo, 1941.

Niigata ken nōkai. *Jinushi kosaku mondai ni taisuru jinushi no iken* [Landlord Opinions on the Landlord-Tenant Problem]. Niigata, 1921.

Niwa Kunio. *Keisei ki no Meiji jinushi sei* [The Formative Period of the Meiji Landlord System]. Tokyo, 1964.

Nōchi kaikaku kiroku iinkai. *Nōchi kaikaku tenmatsu gaiyō* [Detailed Summary of the Land Reform]. Tokyo, 1951.

Nōchi seido shiryō shūsei hensan iinkai. *Kosaku sōgi ni kansuru shiryō* [Materials on Tenancy Disputes], vol. 2 of *Nōchi seido shiryō shūsei* [Collected Materials on the Agricultural Land System]. Tokyo, 1969.

Nōmin undō shi kenkyū kai. *Nihon nōmin undō shi* [History of the Farmers' Movement in Japan]. Tokyo, 1961.

Nōrinshō, daijin kanbō, tōkeika. *Nōrinshō tōkei hyō* [Statistics of the Ministry of Agriculture and Forestry]. Tokyo, 1931.

Nōrinshō, nōmukyoku. *Chihō betsu kosaku sōgi gaiyō* [Regional Summary of Tenancy Disputes], vols. 2 and 3. Tokyo, 1934 and 1936.

————. *Honpō nōgyō yōran* [Survey of Japanese Agriculture]. Tokyo, 1940.

————. *Jinushi kosakunin kumiai kiyaku jirei* [Examples of the Bylaws of Landlord and Tenant Unions]. Tokyo, May 1926.

————. *Jinushi kosakunin kumiai undō no gaiyō* [Summary of the Landlord and Tenant Union Movements]. Tokyo, August 1928.

————. *Kosaku nenpō* [Annual Report on Tenancy], 1926–1935. Tokyo, 1926–1935.

————. *Kosaku sōgi no gaikyō* [The General Nature of Tenancy Disputes]. Tokyo, 1928.

————. *Kosaku sōgi oyobi chōtei jirei* [Examples of Tenancy Disputes and Their Arbitration], vol. 9, 1934. Tokyo, 1936.

————. *Nōchi kankei tochi gaisha oyobi ukeoi kosaku ni kansuru chōsa* [Survey of Agricultural Land Companies and Contract Tenancy]. Tokyo, December 1932.

_____. *Nōchi nenpō* [Annual Report on Agricultural Land], 1940–41. Tokyo, 1942.

Nōshōmushō, daijin kanbō, tōkeika. *Nōshōmushō tōkei hyō* [Statistics of the Ministry of Agriculture and Commerce]. Tokyo, 1921.

Nōshōmushō, nōmukyoku. *Jinushi kumiai ni kansuru chōsa* [Survey of Landlord Unions]. Tokyo, August 1921.

_____. *Kosaku sōgi ni kansuru chōsa* [Survey of Tenancy Disputes]. 2 vols. Tokyo, 1922.

Ogura Takekazu. *Tochi rippō no shiteki kōsatsu* [An Historical Study of Land Legislation]. Tokyo, 1951.

Oikawa Shirō, ed. *Yamagata ken nōchi kaikaku shi* [History of the Land Reform in Yamagata Prefecture]. Yamagata, 1953.

Okayama ken naimubu. *Okayama ken kosaku kankō chōsa sho* [Survey of Tenancy Practices in Okayama Prefecture]. Okayama, 1924.

Okutani Matsuji. *Kindai Nihon nōsei shiron* [An Historical Treatise on Modern Japanese Agricultural Policy]. Tokyo, 1938.

Ono Takeo. *Meiji zenki tochi seido shiron* [History of the Land System in the Early Meiji Era]. Tokyo, 1948.

_____. *Nōson shi* [A History of Rural Villages], vol. 9 of *Gendai Nihon bunmei shi* [The History of Modern Japanese Culture]. Tokyo, 1941.

Ōuchi Tsutomu. *Nōgyō mondai* [Agricultural Problems]. Tokyo, 1961.

Sunaga Shigemitsu, ed. *Kindai Nihon no jinushi to nōmin* [Landlords and Farmers of Modern Japan]. Tokyo, 1966.

Takahashi Kamekichi. *Meiji Taishō nōson keizai no hensen* [Changes in the Rural Economy in Meiji and Taishō]. Tokyo, 1926.

Tōbata Seiichi. *Ichi nōsei gakuto no kiroku* [Notes of a Student of Agricultural Policy]. Tokyo, 1947.

_____. *Nihon shihonshugi no keisei sha* [The Builders of Japanese Capitalism]. Tokyo, 1964.

_____. *Nōchi o meguru jinushi to nōmin* [Landlords and Farmers Throughout the Countryside]. Tokyo, 1947.

Tsuchiya Takao. *Meiji zenki keizai shi kenkyū* [An Historical Study of the Early Meiji Economy]. vol. 1. Tokyo, 1944.

Yagi Yoshinosuke. *Beikoku tōsei ron* [A Treatise on Rice Control]. Tokyo, 1934.

Yamagata ken keizaibu. *Kosaku jijō to nōmin undō* [Tenancy Conditions and the Farmers' Movement]. Yamagata, March 1940.

Yamaguchi Kazuo. *Meiji zenki keizai no bunseki* [An Analysis of the Early Meiji Economy]. Tokyo, 1956.

Yoshioka Kin'ichi. *Kindaiteki nōson no rekishi to jittai* [The History and Actual Condition of Modern Rural Villages]. Tokyo, 1951.

Bibliography

II. Articles in Japanese

Araki Moriaki. "Jinushi sei no tenkai" [The Evolution of the Landlord System]. In *Iwanami kōza Nihon rekishi*, vol. 16, pp. 55–102. Tokyo, 1962.

Arimoto Hideo. "Jinushi wa onozukara kamen o dasseyo" [Landlords Should Be Unmasked]. *Nōsei kenkyū* 3:8 (1924): 26–29.

————. "Kosakunō no zokusuru jinushi sū ni tsuite" [Concerning the Number of Landlords from Whom Tenants Rent Land]. *Teikoku nōkai hō* 11 (October 1921): 9–14.

Asada Kyōji. "Kōtai ki Nihon jinushi sei no sonzai keitai" [The State of the Japanese Landlord System in the Period of Retreat]. *Tochi seido shigaku*, No. 34 (January 1967), pp. 1–20.

Denda Isao. "Kokuminshugi shisō to nōhonshugi shisō" [Nationalism and Agrarianism]. In *Meiji zenhan ki no nashonarizumu*, ed. Sakata Yoshio, 263–309. Tokyo, 1958.

Furushima Toshio. "Meiji Taishō kyōdo shi kenkyū hō" [Research Methods in Meiji-Taishō Local History]. In *Meiji Taishō kyōdo shi kenkyū hō*, ed. Furushima Toshio et al., vol. 7 of *Kyōdo shi kenkyū kōza*, pp. 1–32. Tokyo, 1970.

Furushima Toshio and Morita Shirō. "Meiji ki ni okeru jinushi seido tenkai no chiikiteki seishitsu" [The Regional Nature of the Development of the Landlord System in the Meiji Era]. In *Jinushi sei no keisei*, ed. Meiji shiryō kenkyū renrakukai, pp. 93–120. Tokyo, 1957.

Hayashi Chūtarō. "Kosaku mondai ni kansuru kōsatsu" [A Consideration of the Tenancy Problem]. *Teikoku nōkai hō* 11 (November–December 1921): 26–31, 16–22.

Higashiura Shōji. "Mura no zaisei to fuzai jinushi to no kankei ni tsuite no jirei hitotsu" [An Example of the Relationship between Village Finances and Absentee Landlords]. *Teikoku nōkai hō* 15 (February 1925): 6–8.

Inoue Yūichi. "Jinushi to seinen to no rensa" [The Connections Between Landlords and Youth]. *Teikoku nōkai hō* 2 (March 1912): 20–22.

Kitazaki Susumu. "Tochi kokuyūan no kachi" [The Value of the Proposals to Nationalize Land]. *Chūgai zaikai* 2:4 (1927): 52.

"Kizokuin tagaku nōzeisha giin gosensha ni tsuite" [On the High Taxpayers Elected by Mutual Vote to the House of Peers]. *Teikoku nōkai hō* 8 (July 1919): 60–69.

"Kosaku seido chōsa iinkai" [The Committee to Study the Tenancy System]. *Teikoku nōkai hō* 10 (December 1920): 60–62.

Koyama Magojirō. "Meiji ni okeru jinushi no nōji kairyō undō" [The Landlords' Agricultural Improvement Movement in the Meiji Era]. In

Bibliography

Nihon nōgyō hattatsu shi, ed. Nōgyō hattatsu shi chōsa kai, vol. 5, pp. 599-632. Tokyo, 1955.

Kozei Denzō. "Fuzai jinushi no sonzai kachi ikan" [Concerning the Worth of Absentee Landlords]. *Nōsei kenkyū* 5:9 (1926): 5-12.

Matsukata Masayoshi. "Chisō shi" [History of the Land Tax]. In *Meiji zenki zaisei keizai shiryō shūsei,* ed. Ōkurashō, vol. 1, pp. 365-71. Tokyo, 1933.

Matsumoto Hiroshi. "Meiji Taishō ki ni okeru jinushi no beikoku hanbai ni tsuite" [On Landlord Sales of Rice in the Meiji-Taishō Eras]. *Hitotsubashi ronsō* 60:5 (1968): 547-65.

Mochizuki Shikazō. "Fuzai jinushi bokumetsu saku" [A Policy for Eliminating Absentee Landlords]. *Nōsei kenkyū* 5:9 (1926): 19-22.

Mori Eikichi. "Kaikyū ishiki to kumiai undō' [Class Consciousness and the Union Movement]. *Nōsei kenkyū* 3:7 (1924): 61-64.

Nishida Yoshiaki, "Kosaku sōgi no tenkai" [The Evolution of Tenancy Disputes]. In *Meiji Taishō kyōdo shi kenkyū hō,* eds. Furushima Toshio et al., vol. 7 of *Kyōdo shi kenkyū kōza,* pp. 346-69. Tokyo, 1970.

————. "Nōchi kaikaku no rekishiteki seikaku" [The Historical Character of the Land Reform]. In *Rekishi ni okeru minzoku to minshushugi,* Rekishigaku kenkyū kai (November 1973): 159-74.

Nomura Shinshichi. "Fuzai jinushi kanarazu shimo haisubekarazu" [Absentee Landlords Should Not Necessarily Be Eliminated]. *Nōsei kenkyū* 5:9 (1926): 24-25.

Nōrinshō, nōmukyoku. "Gojitchōbu ijō no kōchi o shoyū suru ōjinushi ni kansuru chōsa (1925)" [Survey of Large Landlords Owning Fifty or More *Chō* of Land]. In *Nihon nōgyō hattatsu shi,* ed. Nōgyō hattatsu shi chōsa kai, vol. 7, pp. 683-704. Tokyo, 1955.

————. "Gojitchōbu ijō no ōjinushi meibo (1924)" [Register of Large Landlords Owning Fifty *Chō* or More]. In *Nihon nōgyō hattatsu shi,* ed. Nōgyō hattatsu shi chōsa kai, vol. 7, pp. 705-74. Tokyo, 1955.

Nōshōmushō, nōmukyoku. "Gojitchōbu ijō no ōjinushi ni kansuru chōsa (1921)" [Survey of Large Landlords with Fifty *Chō* or More]. In *Nihon nōgyō hattatsu shi,* ed. Nōgyō hattatsu shi chōsa kai, vol. 7, pp. 671-82. Tokyo, 1955.

Ogawa Makoto. "Chisui suiri tochi kairyō no taikeiteki seibi" [The Rationalization of Flood Control, Irrigation, and Land Improvement]. In *Nihon nōgyō hattatsu shi,* ed. Nōgyō hattatsu shi chōsa kai, vol. 4, pp. 117-232. Tokyo, 1954.

Ogura Takekazu. "Meiji zenki nōsei no dōkō to nōkai no seiritsu" [Early Meiji Trends in Agricultural Policy and the Creation of Agricultural

Associations]. In *Nihon nōgyō hattatsu shi*, ed. Nōgyō hattatsu shi chōsa kai, vol. 3, pp. 219-386. Tokyo, 1954.

Ohashi Hirō. "Gojitchōbu ijō no ōjinushi chōsa oyobi meibo no mondai" [Problems with the Surveys and Registers of Large Landlords Owning Fifty *Chō* or More]. *Chihō shi kenkyū*, No. 52, pp. 51-59.

Okada Munemori. "Saikin ni okeru kosaku sōgi no jōkyō to nōmin kumiai undō no dōkō" [The Nature of Contemporary Tenancy Disputes and Trends in the Farmers' Union Movement]. *Teikoku nōkai hō* 26 (June, July, August, and September 1936): 48-59, 75-86, 37-53, 23-35.

Ono Takeo. "Meiji keizai shi yori mitaru kosaku undō bokkō no genryū" [The Origins of the Sudden Rise of the Tenant Movement as seen from Meiji Economic History]. *Sangyō kumiai*, No. 261 (1927), pp. 1-11.

Ōta Ken'ichi. "Fujita ke no sonzai keitai" [The Fujita Family]. In *Jinya machi no kenkyū: Bitchū Ashimori no baai*, ed. Okayama daigaku kyōiku gakubu shakaika kenkyū shitsu, pp. 170-77. Okayama, n.d.

————. "Setōnaikai engan chiiki ni okeru jinushi sei no dōkō" [Trends in the Landlord System of the Inland Sea Coastal Region]. *Tochi seido shigaku*, No. 27 (n.d. [1954?]), pp. 52-66.

Saitō Eiichi. "Jinushi no zaisan kōsei ni tsuite" [Concerning the Structure of Landlord Property]. *Shakai seisaku jihō*, Nos. 156 and 157 (September and October 1933), pp. 64-76, 74-87.

Saitō Isamu. "Nihon nōmin undō no jiki kubun ni tsuite no shiron" [A Treatise on the Periodization of the Farmers' Movement]. *Keizai kagaku* (1958): 1-85.

Satō Shigemi, "Meiji Taishō ki ni okeru nōgyō gijitsu no hattatsu to haikei: Shōnai chihō no kanden bakō to kōchi seiri o chūshin to shite" [The Background and Development of Agricultural Technology in the Meiji and Taishō Periods: The Case of Dry-Field Cultivation and Land Adjustment in the Shōnai Region]. *Nōgyō hattatsu shi chōsakai shiryō*, No. 89 (March 1955).

Shibutani Ryūichi and Ishiyama Shōjirō. "Meiji chūki no jinushi meibo" [Mid-Meiji Landlord Registers]. *Tochi seido shigaku*, No. 30 (June 1966), pp. 54-70.

Sugiyama Motojirō. "Mazu fuzai jinushi o naku seyo" [First Eliminate Absentee Landlords]. *Nōsei kenkyū* 5:9 (1926): 23-24.

"Taishō gannen honpō kosaku kankō chōsa shiryō" [Tenancy Practices in Japan, 1912]. In *Honpō kosaku kankō*, Nōrinshō, nōmukyoku, pp. 1-135. Tokyo, 1926.

"Taishō jūnen honpō kosaku kankō" [Tenancy Practices in Japan, 1921]. In *Honpō kosaku kankō*, Nōrinshō, nōmukyoku, pp. 136-372. Tokyo, 1926.

Teikoku nōkai. "Kosaku sōgi jinushi kosakunin kumiai kosaku chōtei ni kansuru shiryō" [Materials Concerning Tenancy Disputes, Landlord and Tenant Unions, and Tenancy Arbitration]. *Teikoku nōkai hō* 27 (June 1937): 359-76.

Teikoku nōkai, chōsabu. "Kosaku sōgi ni kansuru chōsa" [Survey of Tenancy Disputes]. *Teikoku nōkai hō* 12 (June 1922): 39-46.

Tōbata Seiichi. "Nihon nōgyō hatten no ninaite" [The Agents of Agricultural Development in Japan]. In *Nihon nōgyō hattatsu shi,* ed. Nōgyō hattatsu shi chōsa kai, vol. 9, pp. 561-604. Tokyo, 1956.

Toyama Shinzō. "Fuzai jinushi to kazei" [Absentee Landlords and Taxation]. *Teikoku nōkai hō* 6 (October 1916): 36-40.

Wagatsuma Tōsaku. "Jinushi seido to buraku seido to no kankei" [Connections Between the Landlord System and the *Buraku* System]. *Teikoku nōkai hō* 33 (May 1943): 1-10.

Watanabe Shin'ichi. "Rōdō ichiba no hatten to kosaku kankei" [The Development of the Labor Market and Tenancy Relations]. *Nōgyō to keizai* 4:1 (1937): 10-20.

Yamada Ken. "Sōsenkyo ni taisuru nōgyōsha no kakugo" [The Readiness of Farmers for the General Election]. *Teikoku nōkai hō* 10 (April 1920): 8-14.

Yokoi Tokiyoshi. "Jinushi no seikatsu" [The Life of Landlords]. *Chūō nōji hō,* No. 63 (June 1905), pp. 1-3.

III. *Other Japanese Sources*

1. *Interviews*

Baba Akira, professor, Tohoku University, Sendai, Miyagi Prefecture, 28 May 1967.

Hattori Waichirō, businessman and former landlord, Ushimado, Ōku *gun,* Okayama Prefecture, 15 May 1967.

Hoshijima Gihei, principal, Sanyō Gakuen, Okayama Prefecture and former landlord, 16 May 1967.

Itō Bunkichi, former landlord, Somi, Nakakambara *gun,* Niigata Prefecture, 9 August 1967.

Kubo Yasuo, Niigata Prefecture Agricultural Construction Office, Niigata, 10 August 1967.

Namba Giichirō, steward to Nōzaki family, former landlords, Ajino, Kojima *gun,* Okayama Prefecture, 14 May 1967.

Tamaki Hisahiko, village official and former landlord, Tagami, Minamikambara *gun,* Niigata Prefecture, 11 August 1967.

Ueno Kyō, village mayor and former landlord, Nango, Tōda *gun.* Miyagi Prefecture, 27 May 1967.

2. *Bibliographies*

Nōrinshō toshokan, ed. *Nōrin bunken kaidai: nōchi mondai hen* [An Annotated Bibliography on Agriculture and Forestry: The Land Problem]. Tokyo, March 1965.

Shibutani Ryūichi, ed. *Jinushi meibo shiryō shozai mokuroku* [Catalogue of Titles and Locations of Landlord Registers]. Tokyo, 1963.

"Tochi mondai bunken ippan" [A Bibliography on the Land Problem]. *Teikoku nōkai hō* 27 (June 1937): 295–327.

IV. *Books and Monographs in English*

Bennett, John W., and Ishino, Iwao. *Paternalism in the Japanese Economy.* Minneapolis, 1963.

Chambliss, William Jones. *Chiaraijima Village: Land Tenure, Taxation, and Local Trade, 1818–1884.* Tucson, 1965.

Cole, Allan B. *Japanese Society and Politics: The Impact of Mobility and Social Stratification.* Boston, 1956.

Dore, Ronald P. *Land Reform in Japan.* London, 1959.

Embree, John. *Suye Mura, A Japanese Village.* Chicago, 1946.

Fukutake, Tadashi. *Japanese Rural Society.* London, 1967.

Grad, Andrew J. *Land and Peasant in Japan: An Introductory Survey.* New York, 1952.

Hagen, Everett Einar. *On the Theory of Social Change: How Economic Growth Begins.* Homewood, Ill., 1962.

Hirschmeier, Johannes. *Entrepreneurship in Meiji Japan.* Cambridge, Mass., 1964.

Mingay, G.E. *English Landed Society in the Eighteenth Century.* London, 1963.

Mitrany, David. *Marx Against the Peasant.* Chapel Hill, N.C., 1951.

Moore, Barrington. *Social Origins of Dictatorship and Democracy: Lord and Peasant in the Making of the Modern World.* Boston, 1967.

Nakamura, James I. *Agricultural Production and the Economic Development of Japan, 1873–1922.* Princeton, 1966.

Robertson Scott, J.W. *The Foundations of Japan.* London, 1922.

Smith, Thomas C. *The Agrarian Origins of Modern Japan.* New York, 1966.

Social Science Research Institute. *The Power Structure in a Rural Community: The Case of Mutsuzawa Mura.* Tokyo, 1960.

Stone, Lawrence. *Crisis of the Aristocracy.* Abridged edition. London, 1967.

Supreme Commander Allied Powers, Natural Resources Section. *Tenancy in Japan.* Tokyo, 1947.

Thompson, F.M.L. *English Landed Society in the Nineteenth Century.* London, 1963.

Bibliography

V. Articles and Papers in English

Dore, Ronald P. "Agricultural Improvement in Japan: 1870-1890." *Economic Development and Cultural Change* 9 (October 1960): 69-91.

———. "Land Reform and Japan's Economic Development." *The Developing Economies* 3 (December 1965): 487-96.

———. "The Meiji Landlord: Good or Bad?" *Journal of Asian Studies* 18 (May 1959): 343-55.

Dore, Ronald, and Ōuchi, Tsutomu. "Rural Origins of Japanese Fascism." In *Dilemmas of Growth in Prewar Japan,* ed. James Morley, pp. 181-209. Princeton, 1971.

Eyre, John D. "The Changing Role of the Former Japanese Landlord." *Land Economics* 31 (February 1955): 35-46.

Kokoris, James A. "The Ōhara Zaibatsu of Okayama." University of Michigan Center for Japanese Studies, *Occasional Papers,* No. 8 (1964), pp. 39-55.

Ladejinsky, Wolf I. "Landlord vs. Tenant in Japan." *Foreign Agriculture* 11 (June 1947): 83-88.

Miller, Helen. "Government Rice Inspection and Tenant Disputes in the Taishō Period" (unpublished paper presented at the Midwest Japan Seminar, December 1972).

Nakamura, James I. "Meiji Land Reform, Redistribution of Income, and Saving from Agriculture." *Economic Development and Cultural Change* 14 (July 1966): 428-39.

Ohkawa, Kazushi, and Rosovsky, Henry. "A Century of Economic Growth." In *The State and Economic Enterprise in Japan,* ed. William Lockwood, pp. 47-92. Princeton, 1965.

Orchard, Dorothy. "Agrarian Problems of Modern Japan." *Journal of Political Economy* 37 (April and June 1929): 129-49, 285-311.

Ranis, G. "Financing of Japanese Economic Development." *Economic History Review* 9 (April 1959): 440-54.

Singer, Kurt. "Landlords and Tenant Farmers of Japan." *Economic Record* 23 (December 1947): 238-49.

Smith, Thomas C. "The Japanese Village in the Seventeenth Century." *The Journal of Economic History* 12 (Winter 1952): 1-20.

———. "Landlords' Sons in the Business Elite." *Economic Development and Cultural Change* 9 (October 1960): 93-108.

Wakukawa, Seiyei. "The Japanese Farm Tenancy System." In *Japan's Prospect,* ed. D.G. Haring, pp. 115-73. Cambridge, Mass., 1946.

Waswo, Ann. "The Origins of Tenant Unrest." In *Japan in Crisis: Essays on Taishō Democracy,* eds. B. Silberman and H. Harootunian, pp. 374-94. Princeton, 1974.

149

Index